Introduction

'Painting and engraving modern moral subjects … my picture was my stage'

Autobiographical Notes, William Hogarth

William Hogarth was a celebrity in his lifetime and, nearly 350 years after his death, his rich and closely observed images still draw visitors from across the world to his country home in Chiswick. Without his enduring fame it is unlikely that Hogarth's House would still be standing. It narrowly avoided being demolished for suburban housing development in 1900, and survived severe bomb damage in 1940 and a decade of neglect before it was put back together and reopened.

This is the story of Hogarth's House – its origins, owners and occupiers. New research undertaken for the refurbishment of 2009–11 has made possible a new presentation of the house, revealing more about the way the house worked as a home and about those who lived there before and after the Hogarths.

We must begin with Hogarth's own story. He was born in Bartholomew Close, near to Smithfield's marketplace, in 1697. In this dog-legged lane his father, Richard Hogarth, found lodgings when he came to London from Westmorland. A school-teacher, he published an introduction to Latin, Greek and English in 1689 and a dictionary in 1691. He married Anne Gibbons, his landlord's daughter, in 1690, and they continued to live in the Gibbons family home. Later Richard ran a school there and supplemented his income working for publishers.

◀ Bartholomew Close, where Hogarth grew up, seen from Duke Street, Smithfield, watercolour of 1852.

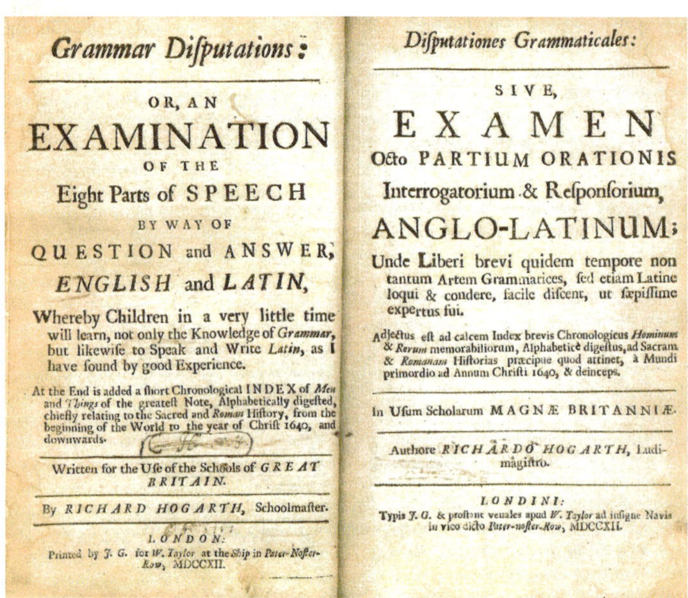

Richard Hogarth's primer in English and in Latin, 1712, with questions and answers for repetition by schoolmaster and pupils.

William was the fifth of nine children, but only he and his two sisters grew to adulthood. Richard Hogarth's Latin-speaking coffee house at St John's Gate was advertised in 1704, but it did not prosper. When William was ten his father was sent to the Fleet Prison for debt. By 1709 Richard had scraped together the five guineas needed to move with his family into one of the lodging houses within the Rules of the Prison. There Anne Hogarth made her ointment for children while her husband ran a school.

New legislation saw Richard Hogarth set free in September 1713, and in the following year William was apprenticed to Ellis Gamble, a silver plate engraver. A relative of his uncle by marriage, Gamble probably waived the apprenticeship fee. William had been well educated by his father; he was able to include in his works numerous biblical references, classical mottoes and symbols and some French phrases.

Anne Hogarth's advertisement for her Gripe Ointment for young children, from *The Daily Courant*, 13 January 1709.

In pity to Infants that cannot tell their Ails, there is now publish'd (having been many Years in private Practice) a most Noble and very safe Medicine, call'd, The GRIPE OINTMENT, which by outward Use only, and in the very moment of Application, Cures the GRIPES in Young Children; and prevents FITS, one half Crown Pot whereof will bring up a Child past all danger from either. Sold only by Mrs. Anne Hogarth next Door to the Ship in Black and White Court, Old-Bailey.

Hogarth's House

'FOUR Miles from Town. –
To be SOLD, a small but highly
respectable HOUSE, well
known as the Residence of the
Celebrated HOGARTH,
pleasantly situated at Chiswick,
in an excellent garden walled
round, well planted, in which
is also a fine walnut and
mulberry tree.'

The Morning Chronicle,
29 April 1814

▶ Miniature portrait of Hogarth
by Jean André Rouquet, enamel on
copper, about 1745.

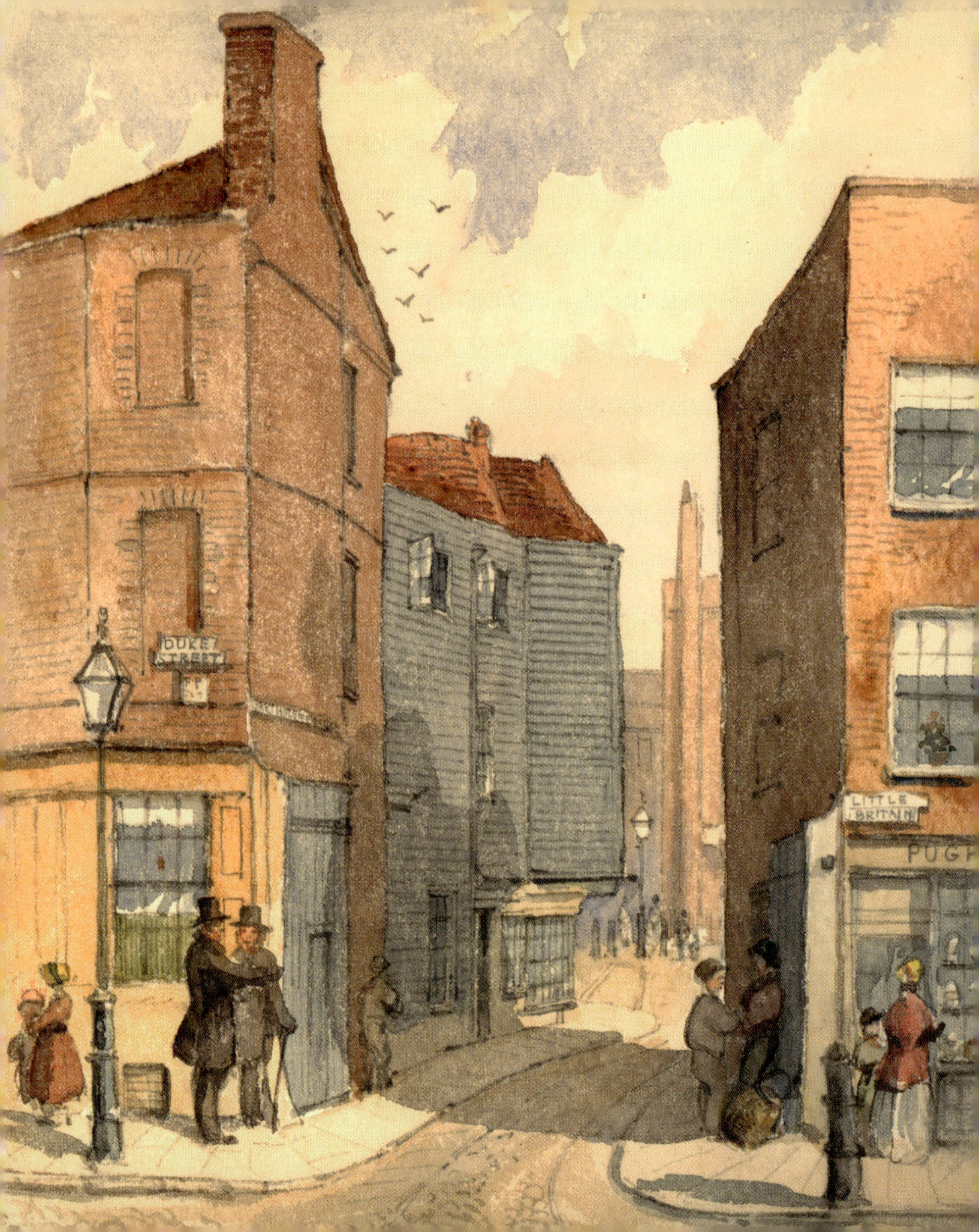

DUKE STREET
LITTLE BRITAIN
PUG

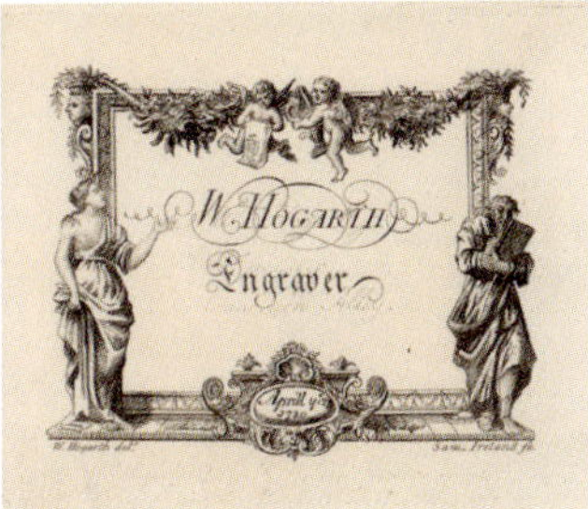

▲ Hogarth's elegant trade card, dated 23 April 1720 – St George's Day, the birthday of his hero, William Shakespeare.

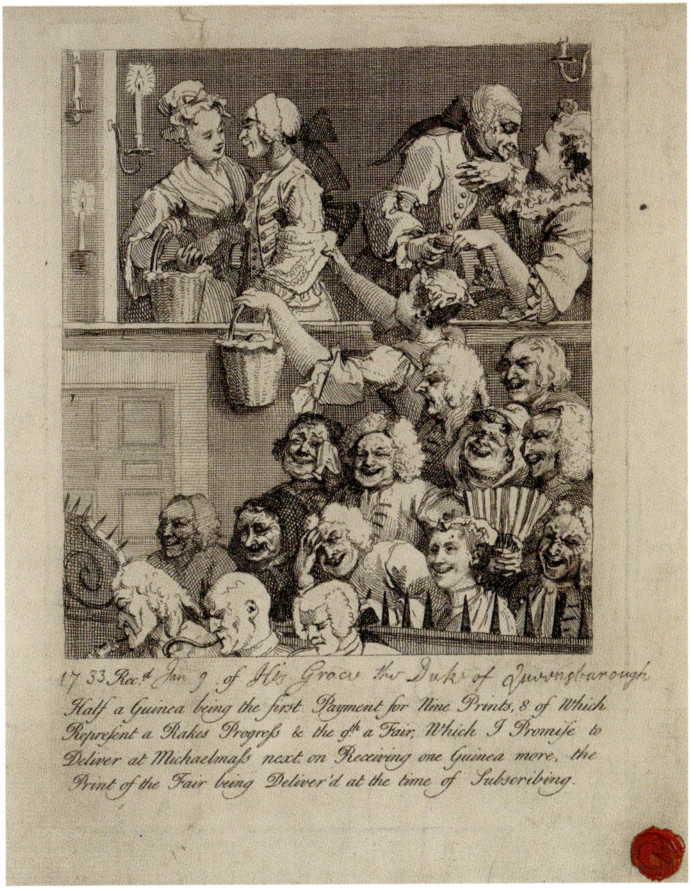

▶ Subscribers to Hogarth's *The Rake's Progress*, 1733, received this receipt, with an image of *The Laughing Audience* and the artist's seal impression.

Hogarth gave up his apprenticeship in 1717. He began producing illustrations and satirical images for printseller-publishers. He later wrote: 'Engraving on copper was, at twenty years of age, my utmost ambition'. The 1720s were formative years during which Hogarth nurtured his talent. He joined the new artists' academy in St Martin's Lane in 1720, where he made lifelong friends. Some were earning a living as scene painters, and Hogarth grew to love their theatrical world. He joined drinking and dining clubs and became a Freemason.

Infuriated by piracy of his early works, in 1724 Hogarth took the bold step of issuing *Masquerades & Operas* himself, but continued to work with other publishers. He engraved a set of small illustrations for *Hudibras*, Samuel Butler's satirical poem on the English Civil War. Anti-puritan, attacking bigotry and full of oddities, the poem appealed to Hogarth's enjoyment of caricature and his moral sense. In 1725 he prepared a new set of twelve large prints telling the story for print-seller Philip Overton; this was a great success, attracting 192 subscribers. Working on this series, Hogarth chose vivid scenes which moved the story on; this approach was to inform his future series, which he called his 'Modern Moral Subjects'.

Determined to become a history painter, William attended the free academy Sir James Thornhill ran from his home and studio in Covent Garden. Thornhill's son, John, became a close friend. Through his new contacts Hogarth began to win commissions for conversation pieces – group paintings of families or friends. In 1728 William eloped with his mentor's daughter, Jane. Though her parents were soon reconciled to the marriage, Hogarth was not the wealthy husband they might have hoped for.

Like many contemporary artists and writers, Hogarth wanted to satirise the governing party while at the same time hoping for court patronage. He sniped at courtiers who promoted Italianate taste, including Lord Burlington and his protégé, William Kent. Hogarth's training with Gamble enabled him to undertake a major commission in 1728. He engraved a magnificent silver salver made by Paul de Lamerie, commemorating Sir Robert Walpole's service as Chancellor of the Exchequer.

The theatre helped determine Hogarth's style of presentation and was the subject of some of his works. In 1729 he painted John Gay's *The Beggar's Opera*, which delighted audiences of all classes, mixing slang, jokes, symbolism and satire. John Rich made a fortune from it, which he invested in a new Covent Garden theatre and a large version of Hogarth's painting to hang there.

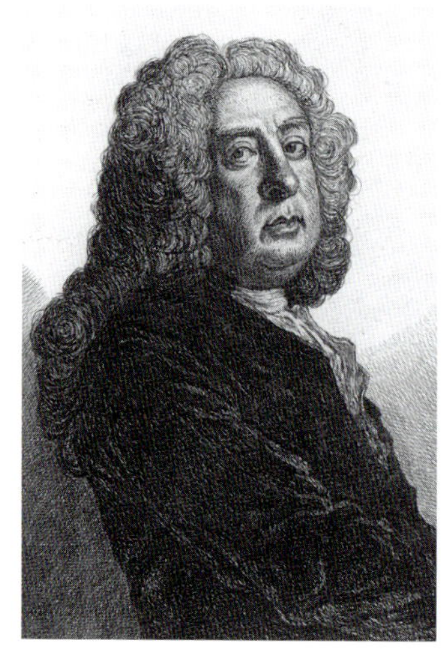

▼ Sir James Thornhill (1676–1734), Sergeant-Painter to the King and Hogarth's father-in-law, etching by Charles Bretherton after a Joseph Highmore portrait of 1732.

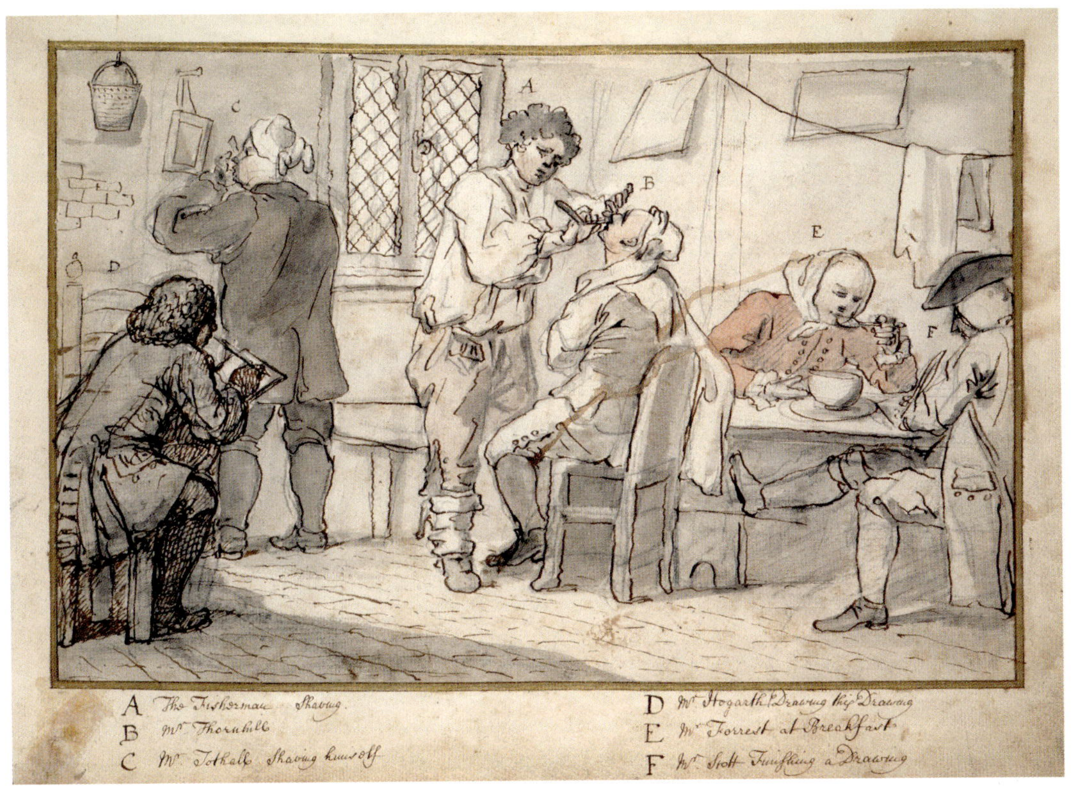

▲ A sketch from the account of the *Five Days' Peregrination*. Hogarth shows himself on the left doing this drawing.

In his thirties, married and beginning to taste success, Hogarth still cherished his circle of friends. In May 1732, after an evening of drinking in the Bedford Arms, he and four others set off on an impromptu Grand Tour, not to the elegant cities of Europe but to the small towns of north Kent. These friends were: John Thornhill, recently appointed Sergeant-Painter to the King in succession to his father; William Tothall, a Covent Garden cloth merchant and Hogarth's neighbour; Ebenezer Forrest, a lawyer and playwright; and Samuel Scott, a seascape painter. Forrest wrote an account of their trip, and Hogarth provided ten sketches of their adventures, including a boat trip, sightseeing, food and drink, accommodation and even a game of hopscotch!

The publication of *A Harlot's Progress* in 1732 made Hogarth a significant and well-known artist. While his *Hudibras* series had used Samuel Butler's story, in this first 'Modern Moral Subject' both the story and imagery were Hogarth's own. He showed the paintings in his studio and advertised the prints for sale by subscription, cutting out the publishers to keep the profits for himself – and assembling a list of potential future buyers.

He sold 1,240 sets of the prints, which brought him some financial security, funds to buy a townhouse in Leicester Fields and a business that would continue to support his widow after his death. The injustice of piracy still irked him. Before publishing his next series, *The Rake's Progress*, he and a group of colleagues petitioned Parliament for legislation to protect artists' copyright in their work.

▶ *The Painter and his Pug*, Hogarth's self-portrait of 1745, probably John Leighton's copy donated by him in 1904.

▼ The Hogarths' house at the south-east corner of Leicester Fields (now Leicester Square) when it was a hotel in 1801.

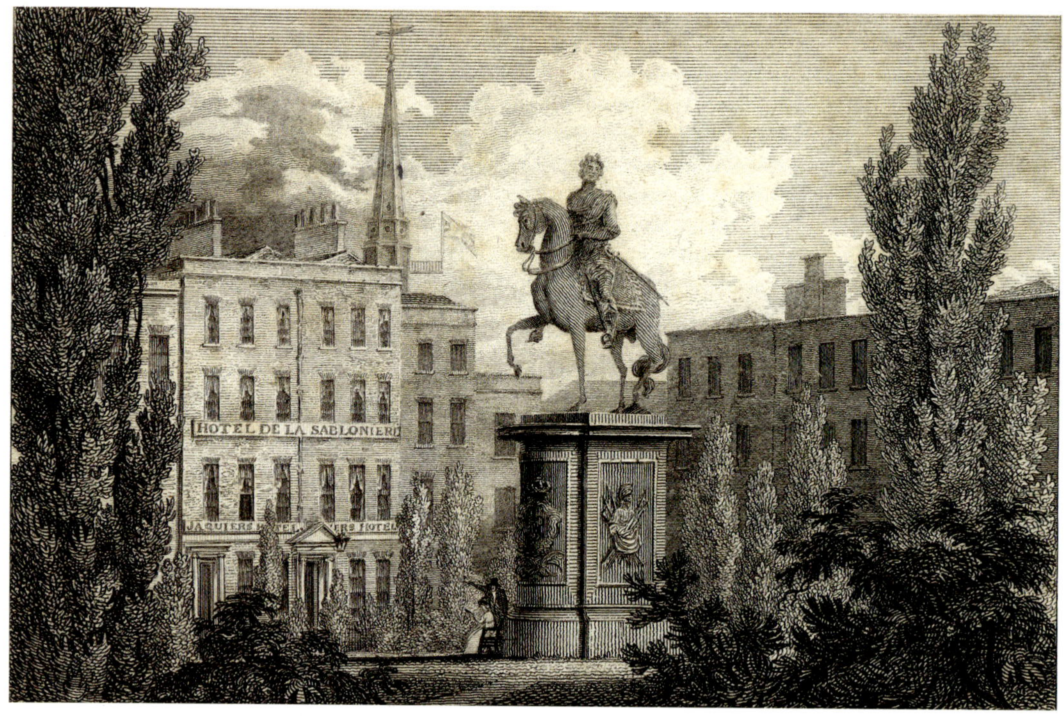

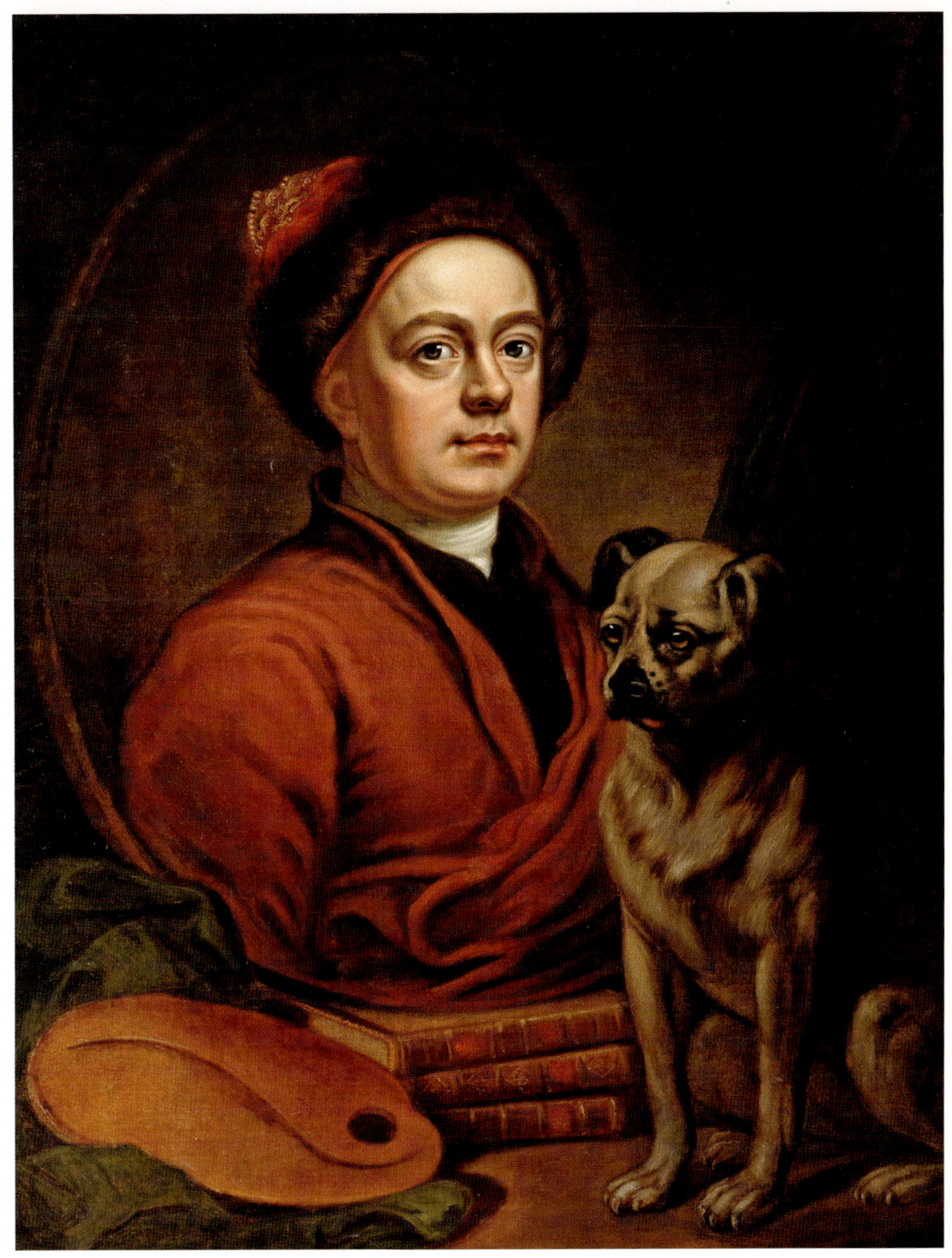

When Thornhill died in 1734 Hogarth inherited his studio furniture and equipment, enabling him to reopen the St Martin's Lane academy. There he rejected the usual veneration of Old Master paintings and emphasised the value of drawing from life, developing the theory of art which would appear in his book, *The Analysis of Beauty*. He still aspired to follow Thornhill as a history painter. When Amigoni, a Venetian artist who had been Thornhill's rival, was about to be commissioned to provide paintings for the grand staircase of St Bartholomew's Hospital, Hogarth seized the opportunity, offering to do the work without charge. He combined philanthropy with a little self-promotion.

Soon Hogarth was supporting Thomas Coram's campaign for a Foundling Hospital to care for the numerous abandoned babies in London, becoming a founding governor. He donated a stunning portrait of Coram and encouraged artist friends to give paintings, attracting visits from potential supporters. Later he supervised the Hospital's wet nurses in Chiswick.

▼ A drawing by Hogarth that was used to solicit support for the Foundling Hospital, 1739.

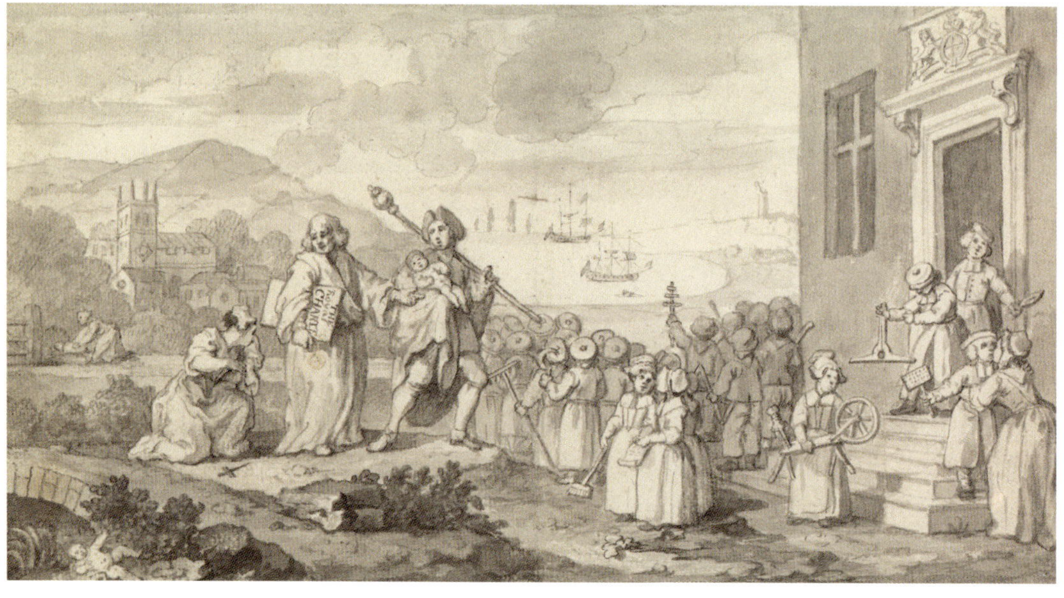

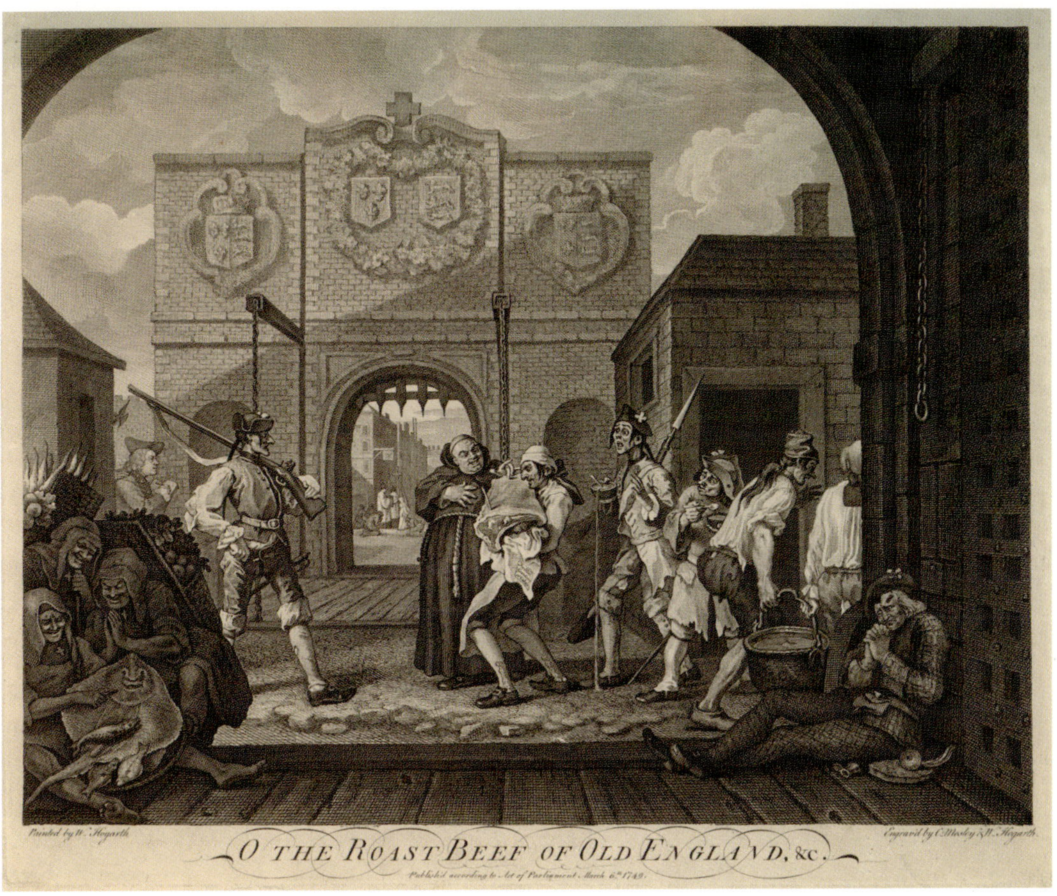

▲ Hogarth's arrest in Calais; he appears extreme left with the arresting officer's hand on his shoulder.

Despite his dislike of continental taste and his animosity towards Amigoni, Hogarth used French engravers to prepare high-quality printing plates for *The Rake's Progress* and *Marriage A-La-Mode*; Gravelot taught at his academy, Rouquet painted his miniature, and Roubiliac sculpted Hogarth's bust and his pug dog. Travelling in France in 1749, however, Hogarth played the role of xenophobic Englishman abroad; outraged at being arrested as a spy, he painted and later engraved the scene in Calais, shamelessly stereotyping the French.

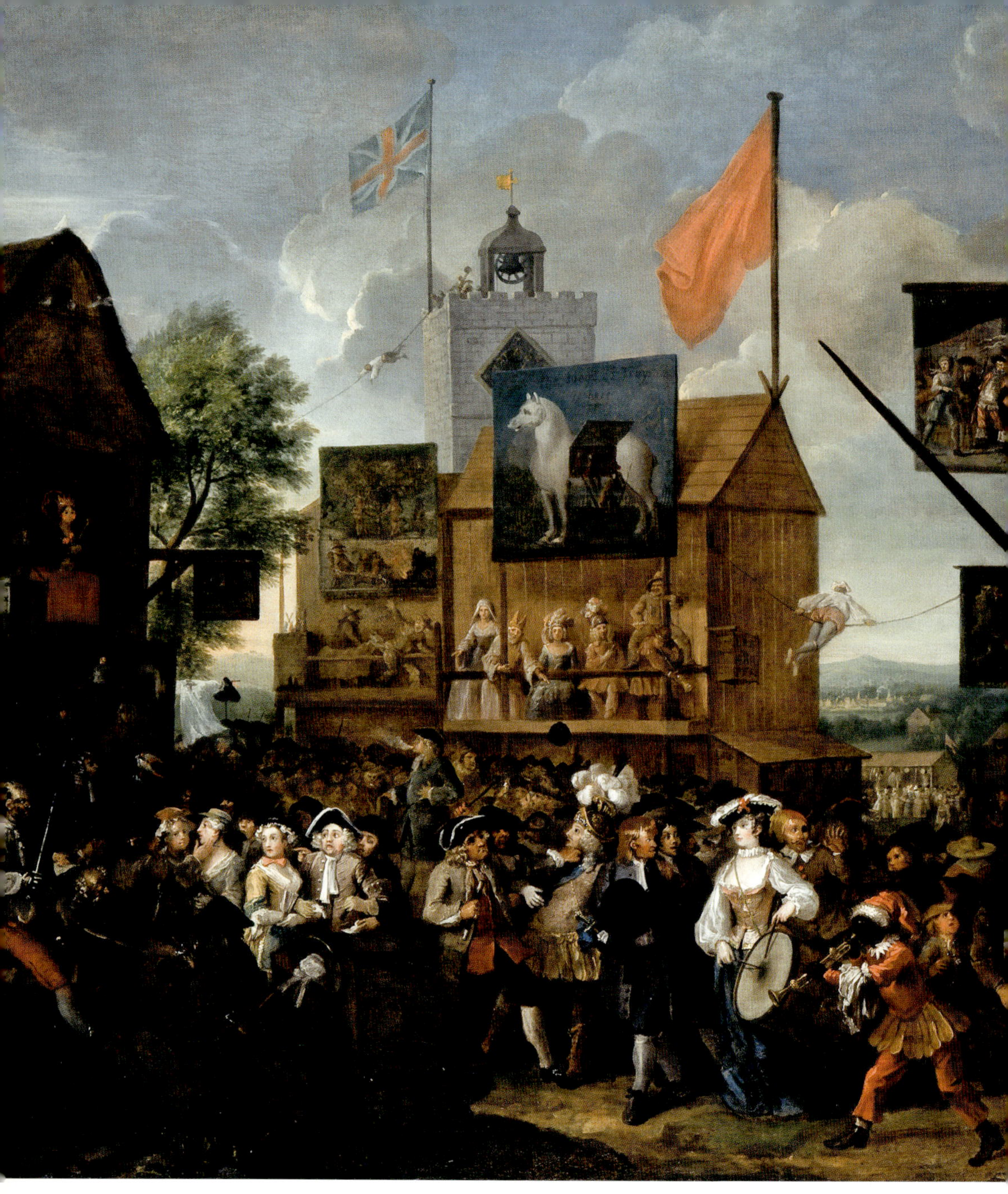

William Hogarth was essentially a London artist. The world's largest city was *his* world, from childhood to old age, through bad times and good. He depended upon London for his work and his pleasure. He moved between friends and fellow artists, patrons and politicians, court officials and the cosmopolitan crowd in the streets. Even at his second home in Chiswick his neighbours included other Londoners with second homes and working people who made their living supplying London's needs.

Many of the settings of incidents in his 'Modern Moral Subjects' would have been familiar to those of his contemporaries who bought his engravings. Bloomsbury church spires, St James's Palace, Sadler's Wells, Covent Garden Great Piazza and London Bridge are recognisable even today. Works depicting prisons and mental asylums, the back rooms of pubs and a cockpit provide us with a glimpse of a London that has gone.

Growing up near Smithfield, William would have known Bartholomew Fair from personal experience, and as a young man he was a keen theatre-goer. He combined these entertainments in the range of exciting and alarming activities that appear in his painting *Southwark Fair*. In Covent Garden Hogarth found himself amongst artisans, shopkeepers and actors as well as the market traders. In 1731 William and Jane had lodgings in the Little Piazza, above the warehouse where William's friend, William Tothall, worked, and a short stroll from her father's house in the north-east corner of the Great Piazza.

Hogarth's images include people of many races who had settled here – Huguenots leaving their chapel, black servants and workers, Italian fops. He portrays children with particular sensitivity and affection, like the trumpeting black boy in the foreground of *Southwark Fair*.

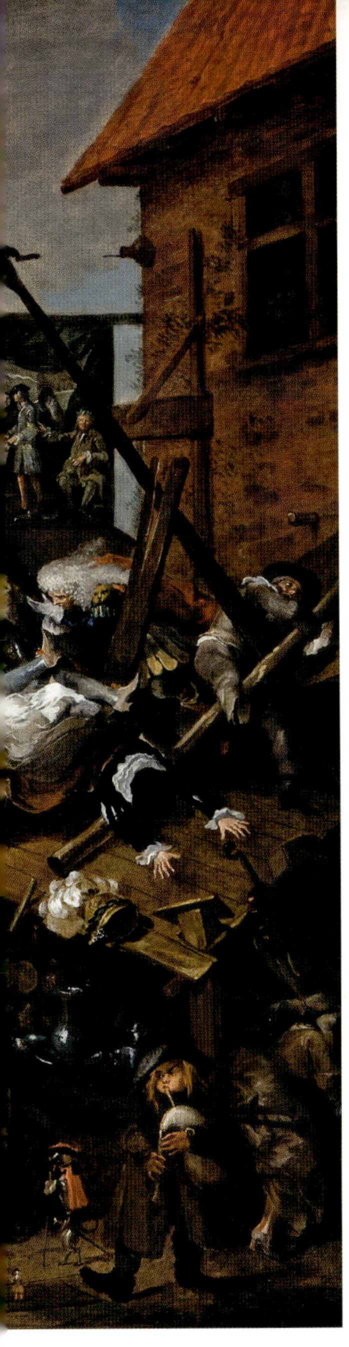

◄ *Southwark Fair*, which was painted in 1732 and issued as a print with *The Rake's Progress*, is an image full of humour, disaster and excitement.

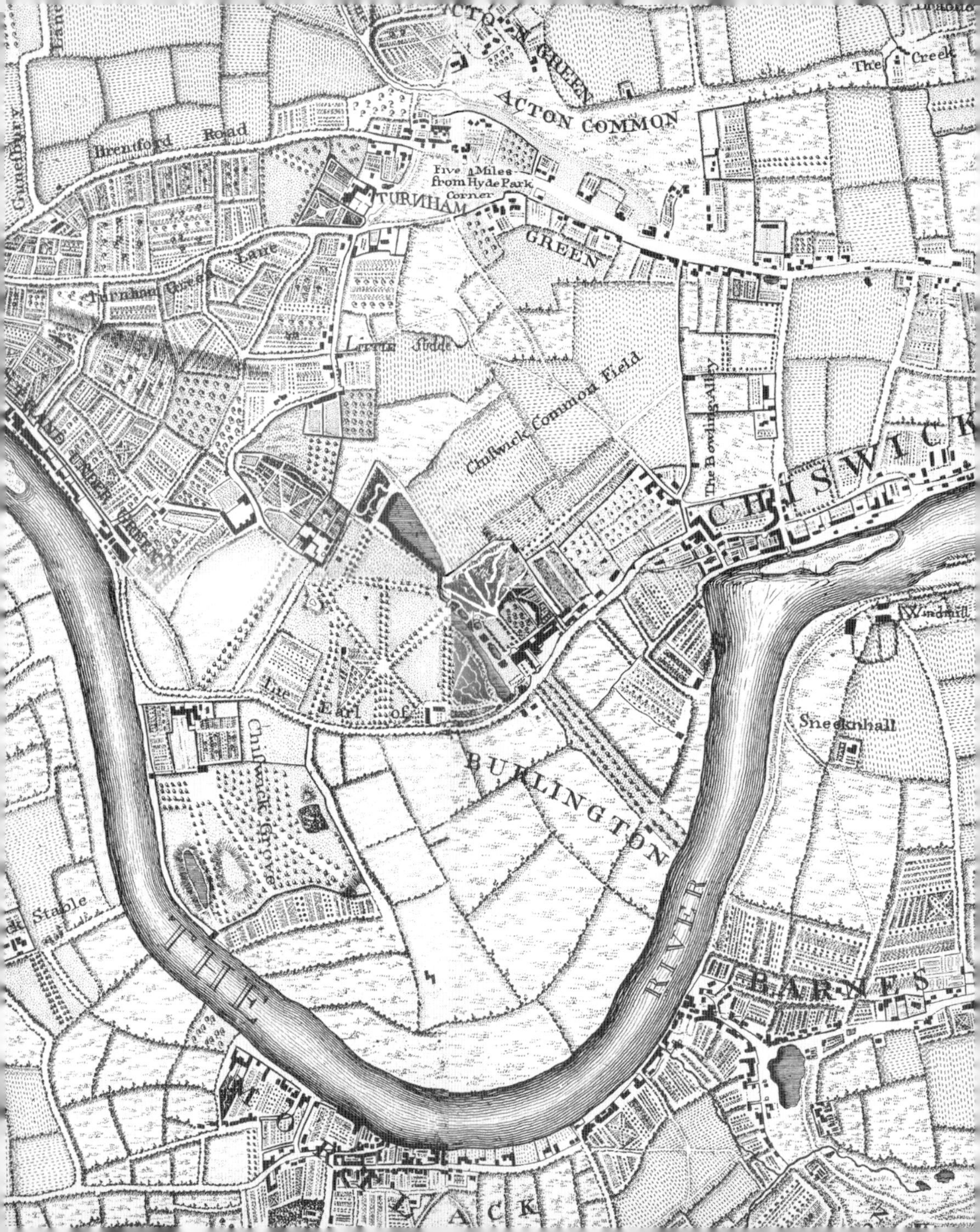
ACTON GREEN
ACTON COMMON
The Creek
Brentford Road
Five Miles from Hyde Park Corner
TURNHAM
GREEN
Turnham Green Lane
Little Sudde
Chiswick Common Field
The Bowling Green Alley
CHISWICK
Chiswick Grove
The Earl of
BURLINGTON
Windmill
Sneednhall
Stable
RIVER
BARNES

1713–1813

'I have found a little country box by the Thames'

From a letter by William Hogarth, 1749

While William Hogarth was serving his apprenticeship, James Downes, a baker, was building the house Hogarth would one day own. The parish accounts record payments to James Downes for communion bread. James' mother, Susannah, died in 1713, leaving him half an acre of land at the north end of Chiswick Town. In the 1680s the manor court had permitted her husband, Richard, to enclose the plot from Chiswick Common Field as an orchard within a brick wall. In one corner James built the new house; the mulberry that grows in its garden may be one of the 1680s fruit trees. Susannah stipulated that her bequests to her children and grandchildren should only be paid after Lady Burlington had settled her large debt to the family business.

Susannah may have chosen the three men who witnessed her will to support this future building project, as they were all involved in the building trade. Abraham Evans lived nearby, and John Meard, his brother-in-law who also lived in Chiswick, developed a large area of Soho. Carpenter Thomas Board regularly repaired St Nicholas' Church and worked for the Burlingtons at Chiswick House and Burlington House in town; Sir Stephen Fox paid him for carpentry in his new Chiswick garden from 1682 until 1684. William Browne came from a family of Brentford brickmakers and gardeners.

◀ Detail of John Rocque's map of *London and Environs*, 1741–45. The house is the last building at the north-west of Chiswick Town, overlooking the Common Field.

By 1717 Georg Andreas Ruperti (1670–1731) was the owner of the new house in Chiswick, a country home for his family away from the bustle of the Savoy where he had been Pastor to the German Lutheran Church since 1706. Ruperti came from the mountainous Harz region of Lower Saxony. He worked with an energetic church council, setting up a school for poor children in 1707 and overseeing building works.

In early 1709 thousands of refugees from the Rhineland were arriving in London. They believed, incorrectly, that Queen Anne would help them establish new lives across the Atlantic. With government funds, Ruperti and Pastor John Tribekko housed over 13,000 refugees in barns and warehouses and compiled a census of them all. When the barns were needed for the harvest, the refugees were moved to camps of army tents at Camberwell and Blackheath. Some refugees eventually went to Ireland, America and Scotland. When a large group returned to their homeland, this finally stopped the mass migration.

Since Queen Anne's husband, Prince George of Denmark, and her successor, George I, brought numerous German officials with them, a Lutheran Court Chapel was created at St James's. From 1711 Ruperti was also its Assistant Pastor, becoming one of its two ministers in 1728 on a generous stipend of £200 a year. During his time in Chiswick Ruperti was a prosperous man.

With his first wife Ruperti had two daughters; in his will he left them a thousand dollars, his late wife's marriage settlement, with her household linen. He left money for his second wife, Anne Elizabeth, in the Brunswick Widows' Cash Fund plus her marriage settlement of one thousand marks. He was desperately concerned that there would be little left for the small children of his second marriage; he asked friends to seek a royal pension to support them and find a position for his young son. Ruperti bequeathed a few books to friends in the Lutheran Church, but directed that they should catalogue the rest of his large library for an auction sale, the proceeds to benefit his family.

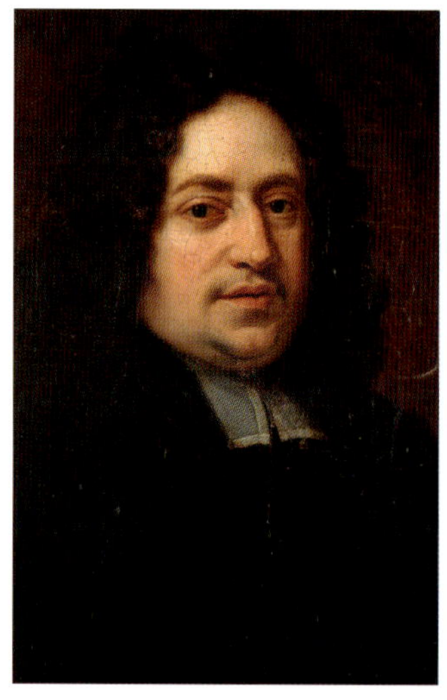

▲ An oil painting of Georg Andreas Ruperti, perhaps from the 1720s, from the Lutheran Church in London.

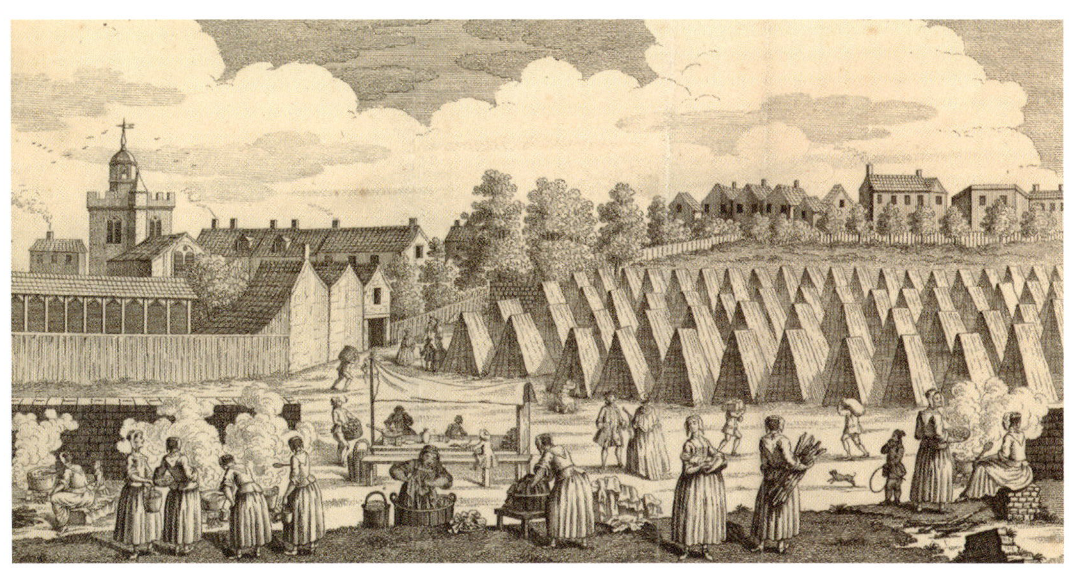

On the same page of *The Daily Journal*, March 20 1732, advertisements appeared for the auction of Ruperti's book collection and for Hogarth's *A Harlot's Progress*. Ruperti's expenditure on books could explain his shortage of funds – 1,090 lots were sold over eight evenings at Covent Garden's Bedford Coffee House, one of Hogarth's haunts. Amidst classical texts and religious commentaries were books on angling and gardening – perhaps some books were for his relaxation in Chiswick.

Ruperti's widow retained the Chiswick house, paying the parish rates, but in 1745 she failed to pay and her name is marked with a P for pauper. *The London Evening Post*, 15 April 1749, reported a 1748 scheme for apprenticing the children of poor clergymen, which included her daughter, Elizabeth, who was placed with Mary Lauch, a mantua-maker in the Savoy. On her son George's twenty-first birthday that same year he inherited the house and put it up for sale. It caught Hogarth's eye – his purchase of a second home in September 1749 probably greatly eased the Rupertis' financial difficulties.

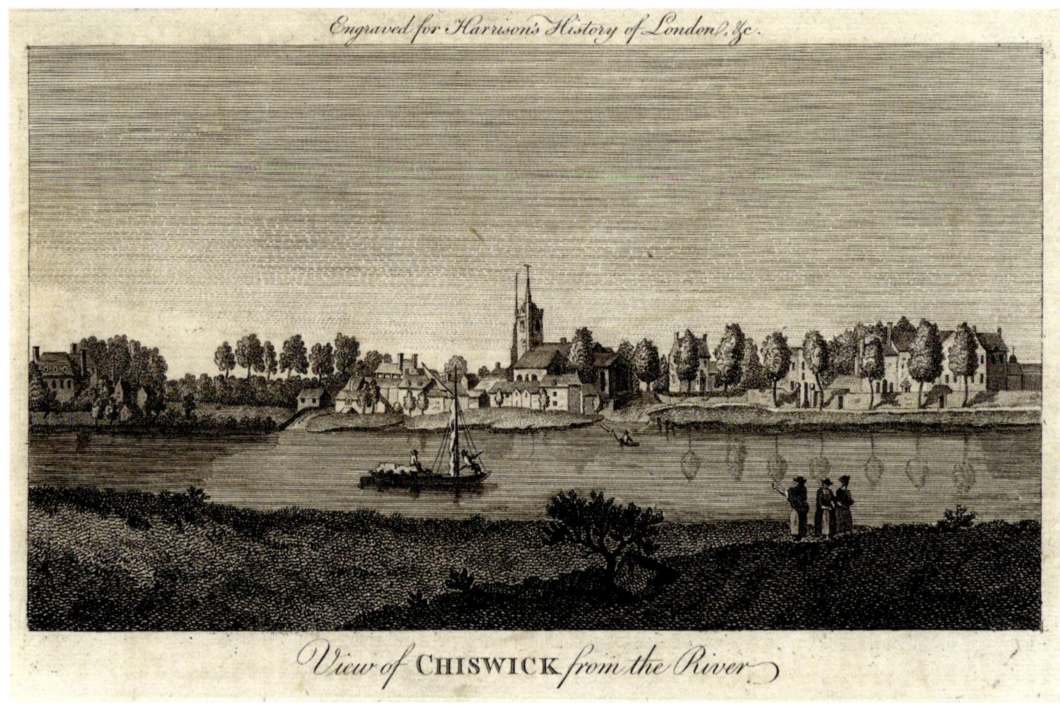

Chiswick parish comprised three prosperous villages, whose residents depended upon fishing, farming, horticulture, brewing and malting. Easily reached by river or road, it offered clean air and rural quiet, so many Londoners kept second homes there. The house stood with its back to Chiswick Town. From its upstairs windows Turnham Green could be seen across the Common Field, straggling along the London-to-Bath road. There inns and blacksmiths served travellers to and from the west of England. Upstream, around the meander of the river, was Strand on the Green.

The Hogarths probably already knew the area. Jane's uncle lived in Twickenham and her cousin in Brentford. The Reverend Thomas Morell (1703–84), one of Handel's librettists and Hogarth's close friend, lived in Turnham Green. Dr John Ranby

▲ Chiswick Town seen from Barnes. The women are waiting for the ferry, plying from the causeway below the parish church.

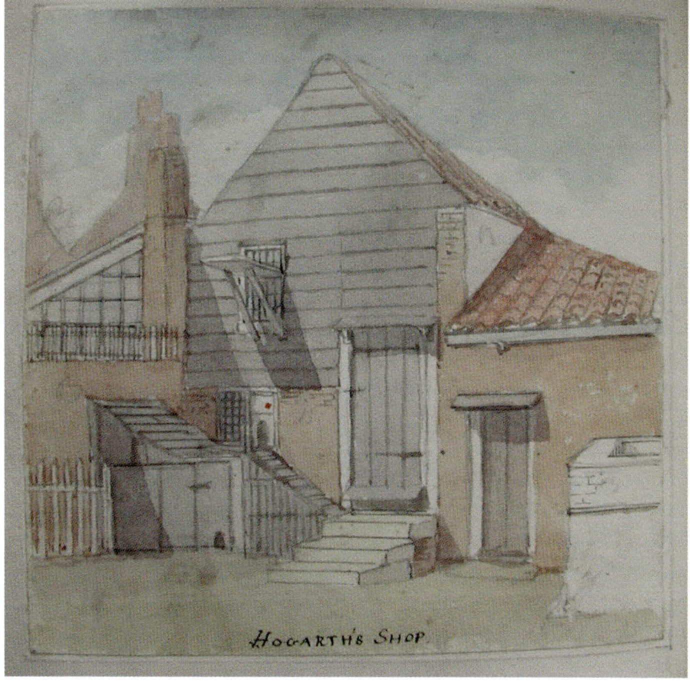

▼ Hogarth's small portable chest for painting pigments and mixing bowls for use when painting away from his studio.

(1703–73), Sergeant-Surgeon to the King, already had a house in Chiswick. Hogarth used him as his model for the Rake in the 1730s and painted beautiful portraits of his children in the 1740s.

Hogarth purchased a three-storey house built from local brick and tiles with wood-panelled walls. It had one room each side of the stairwell, a small cellar and possibly a single-storey lean-to kitchen. The best room had a built-in glazed buffet, fashionable when the house was built. A garden outbuilding provided stabling with a painting room above, where Hogarth could work away from the crowd of women relatives.

The value of the house had fallen from £10 to £7 in the 1740s. It was too small for his whole household, so Hogarth immediately extended it by one room on each floor, and in 1750 the valuation rose again to £10.

The Hogarths' new kitchen had a practical stone floor and stairs to the cellar. The fine reception room over it is loftier than all the others, with more decorative woodwork; to allow for the extra height, two steps lead up into the new bedroom above. These last two rooms have tiny windows at the back, looking towards Chiswick Town. Paint analysis undertaken in 2009 revealed that all the panelling was painted in a wood-pigeon grey before the Hogarth's time, and the extension was painted to match.

Jane presided over a large household, which included her widowed mother, Judith Thornhill until she died in 1757. Jane lived to be eighty, dying in 1789, twenty-five years after her husband. Her cousin and companion, Mary Lewis, continued to help run the print-selling business and eventually inherited the house and the printing plates. Mary's father, David, was a royal harpist and her brother, John, who played the flute, married the sister-in-law of a Clitherow from Boston Manor and lived in Brentford Butts. Mary died aged eighty-eight in 1808.

Hogarth's sisters had a dress shop in Smithfield, then later in Cranbourn Street, near Leicester Fields; Mary died in 1741, but Anne was part of the Chiswick household. She died in 1771 aged seventy and was buried in the family tomb. A wealthy spinster, Julian Bere, also lived with the Hogarths. Like the Thornhills, she had West Country connections, though in her will she asked to be buried near her father at Hammersmith, where her property included the Dove coffee house, now a pub. She left portraits of herself and her parents, probably by Hogarth, as well as diamond earrings for Jane and a Bible for Anne.

At some point the ground floor of the house was remodelled, creating a large room for sociable dinners with the hall to one

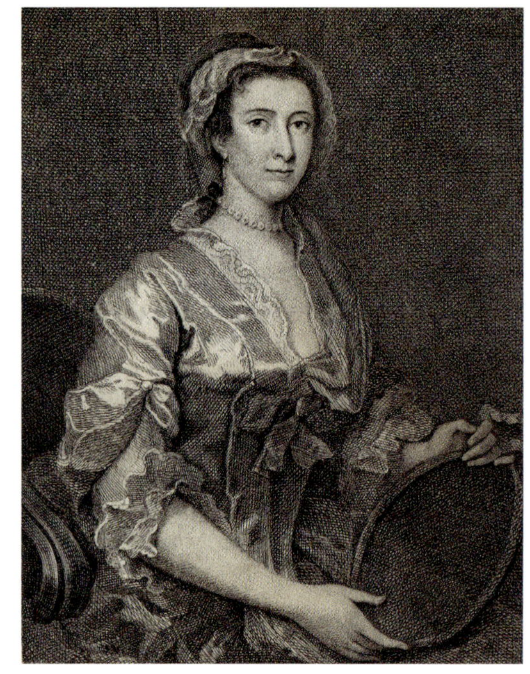

▲ Engraving of Hogarth's portrait of his wife, Jane, about 1738.

▼ Mary Lewis' gold ring set with pearls, a memento of Jane.

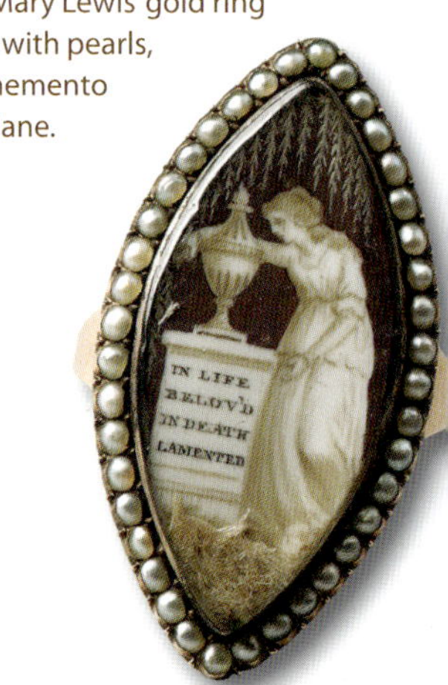

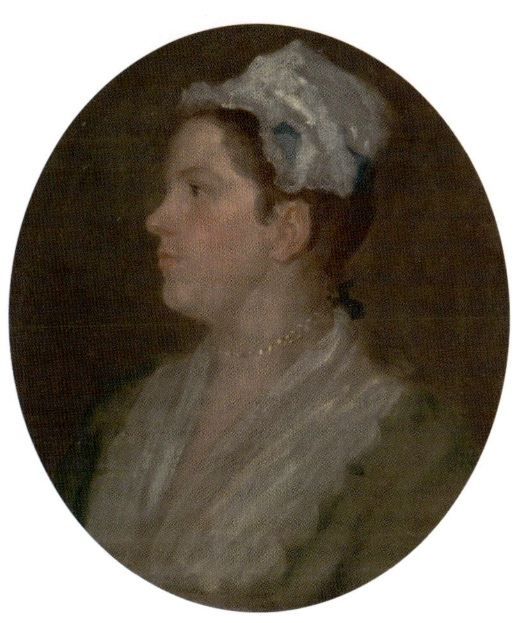

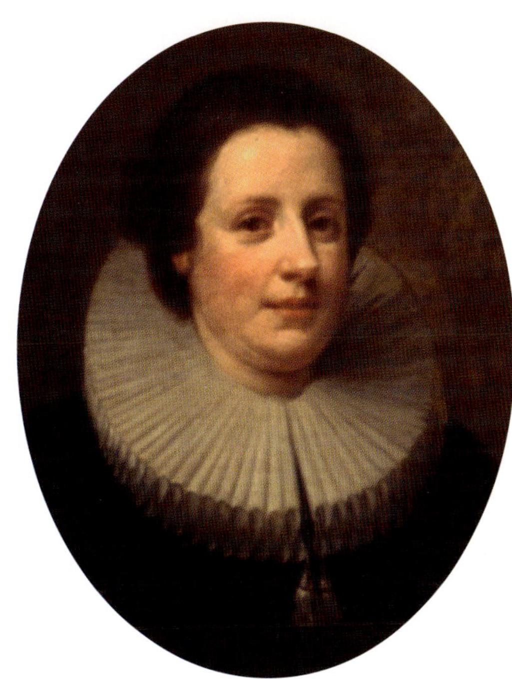

▲ Anne Hogarth, about 1740, one of a pair of portraits of William's sisters, showing the family likeness.

▶ Hogarth's portrait of Mary Lewis in historic dress with a ruff, painted at about the time they came to Chiswick.

side and the stairs behind; all the rooms were repainted in a paler grey. This might have happened in Hogarth's lifetime, but the design of the panelling suggests it was later, in 1770, when Jane added an additional single-storey kitchen wing and the house was revalued at £15.

It is easy to imagine the new room filled with friends, dining or taking tea. Richard Loveday, the surgeon who witnessed Hogarth's will in 1764, lived nearby and must have visited with his daughter, Amelia Jane, Mrs Hogarth's god-daughter. Other visitors included Susanna Woodroffe, from Chiswick Mall, god-mother to Richard's daughter, Catherine. Susanna left mourning rings to Jane, Mary and Julian. Mary Lewis would welcome her brother, John, and his wife, also Mary, as well as the families of their cousins, Mary Hast, whose husband, Philip, was to be Mary Lewis' executor, and Elizabeth Ann Philips.

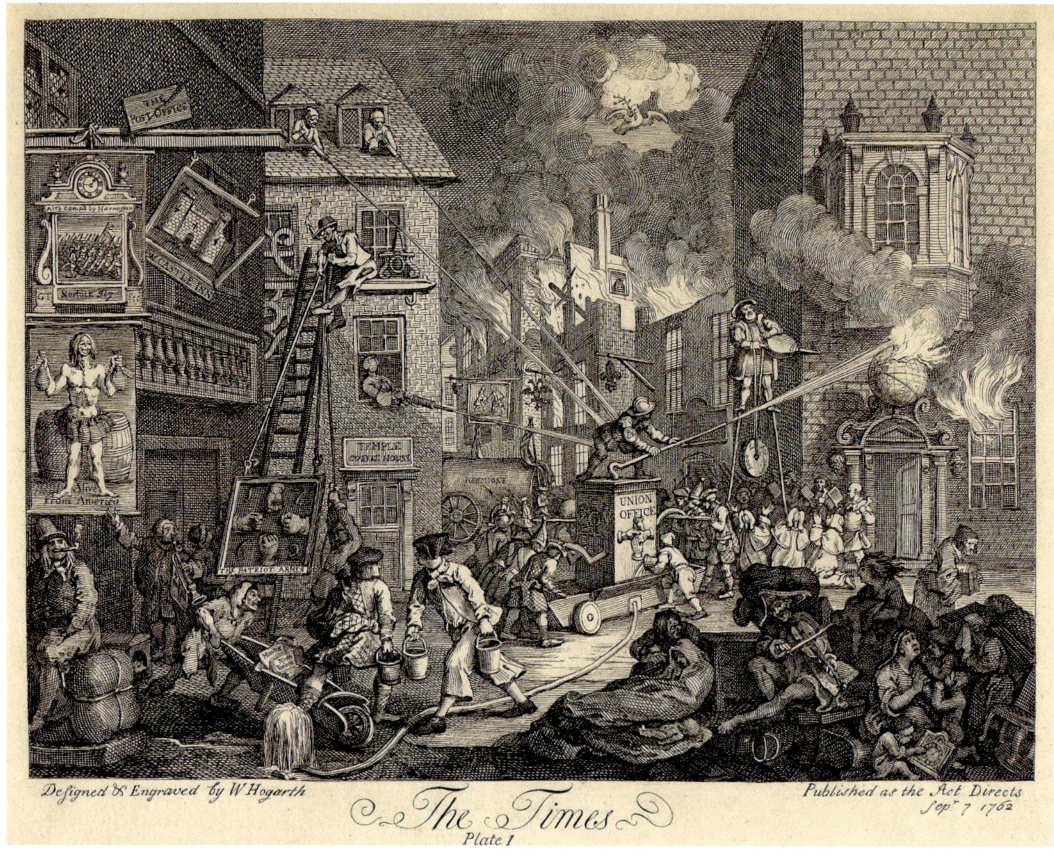

The Times (Plate I), showing Hogarth's oriel window with four little urns (top right), published in 1762.

Hogarth had fifteen happy years at Chiswick, walking with his pug, playing ninepins in his nut walk, working in his painting room, seeing his friends. He sketched the house from across the fields, probably trying out ideas for his extension and certainly before he added the oriel window. This broad bay made the central first-floor room spacious, with views over the garden wall towards the sunset. A window of the same design appears in Hogarth's engraving, *The Times* (Plate I), published in 1762. John Phillips, Jane's nephew, recorded that the pug's drinking bowl stood on a stool beneath the drop-leaf table in the bay window.

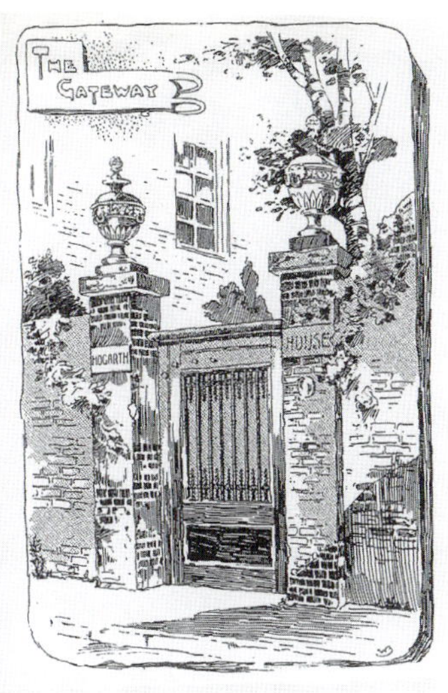

▲ The gate by the house with the fine urns given by actor David Garrick, an illustration of about 1900.

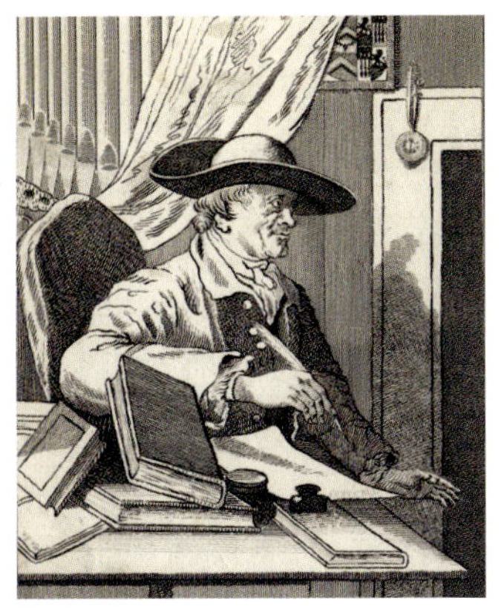

▼ Thomas Morrell, antiquarian, writer and musician, of Turnham Green, in an engraving from Hogarth's portrait, 1762.

In 1745 Hogarth completed a huge portrait of David Garrick, the actor, and issued his largest and most expensive engraving of it, which made Garrick a celebrity. Garrick courted his wife, a protégé of Lord and Lady Burlington, at Chiswick House, and Hogarth painted the couple together. Garrick presented urns for Hogarth's gateposts and in 1771 arranged for the Hogarth family monument to be set up, writing a verse epitaph to Hogarth with Samuel Johnson's help.

Within a short stroll were numerous friends and neighbours. At Turnham Green lived Dr Thomas Morell (1703–84) and his wife, formerly Anne Barker of Chiswick Grove. A classical scholar, Morell was Secretary to the Society of Antiquaries. He wrote elegant libretti for Handel's operas *Judas Maccabeus*, *Theodora* and *Jephtha*. He advised Hogarth on his book, *The Analysis of Beauty*, and asked to be buried near to him.

James Ralph (d. 1762), a writer, came to London with Benjamin Franklin and lived beside the river, next to Whittingham's printing works at the bottom of Chiswick Lane. Arthur Murphy (1727–1805), Irish lawyer, playwright and biographer, also lived along the Thames; he came to the area to be near his friend William Rose, whose boys' boarding school was in Chiswick Lane. Murphy knew the Thrales, one of whom owned Chiswick's Lamb Brewery with John Sich, and introduced them to Samuel Johnson.

Sich was a member of the same masonic lodge in Hammersmith as Richard Loveday (1731–1812). In the 1740s Loveday lived in Chiswick Town but moved to neighbouring Hammersmith for the last forty years of his life. He may have been Hogarth's doctor. His memorial records that 'he practised the art of medicine with the greatest fortune and humanity', describing him as 'straightforward in his ways, generous, sincere and dutiful in his intellect'. Jane Hogarth bequeathed the house to Mary Lewis for her lifetime, and then to Loveday, who inherited in 1808 but only lived until 1812.

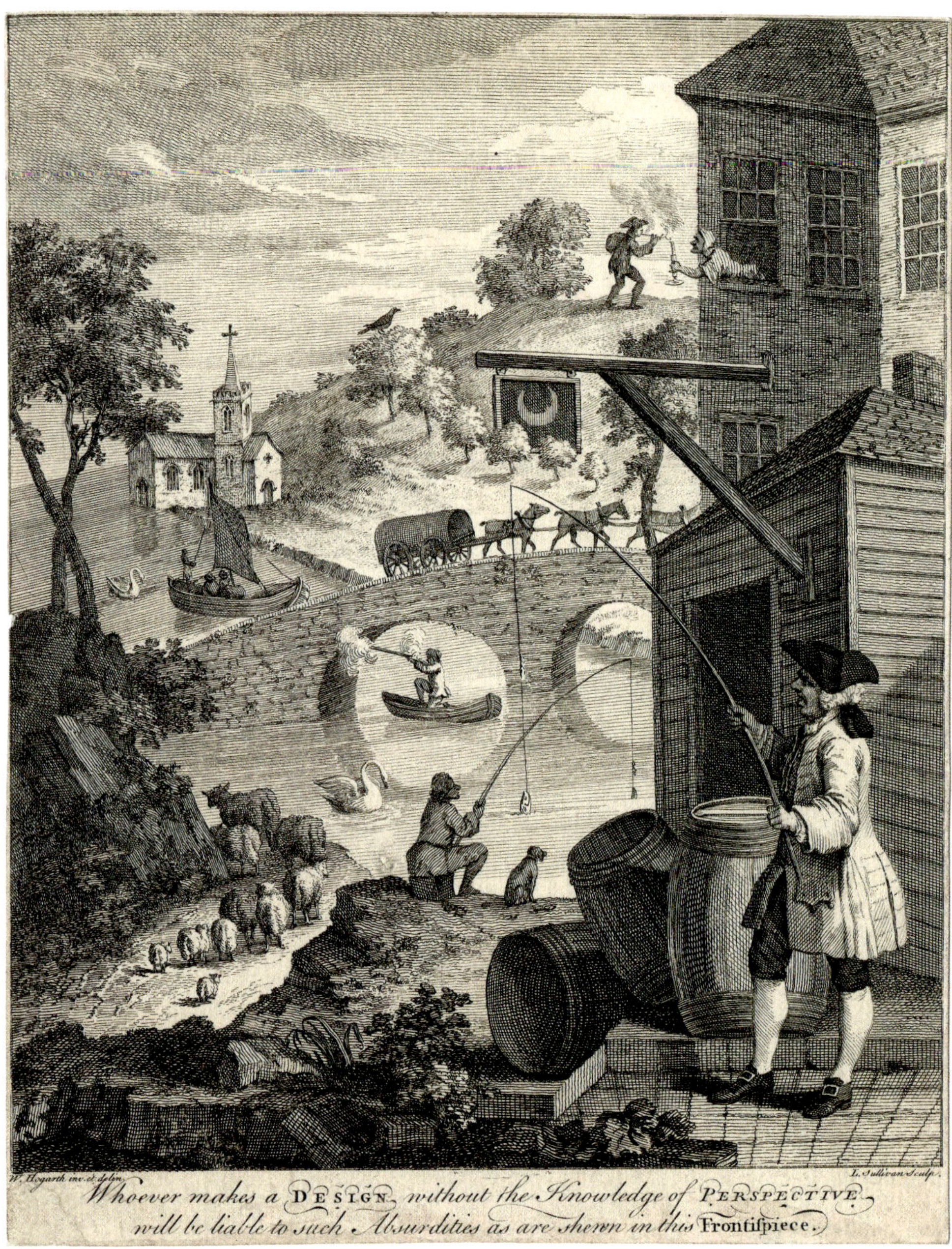

W. Hogarth inv. et delin.
L. Sullivan Sculp.
Whoever makes a DESIGN, without the Knowledge of PERSPECTIVE,
will be liable to such Absurdities as are shewn in this Frontispiece.

24

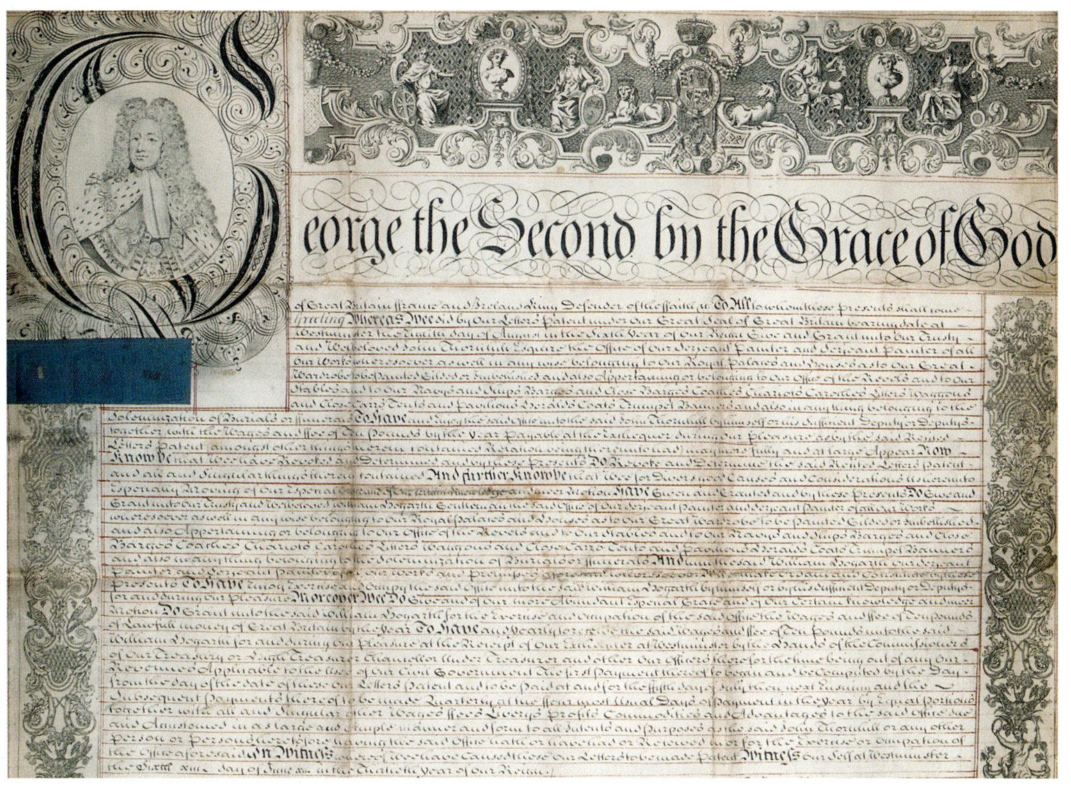

▲ Letters Patent appointing Hogarth Sergeant-Painter, a post in the gift of his neighbour, the Duke of Devonshire, the Lord Chamberlain, 1757.

◄ Hogarth's ingenious frontispiece for Kirby's book, showing how perspective can go awry, 1754.

Joshua Kirby (1716–74) sold Hogarth's prints in Ipswich, and Hogarth encouraged him to paint. In 1754 Kirby published his treatise on *Dr Brook Taylor's Method of Perspective* with illustrations by Hogarth, who advised him on handling opposition to his approach from other artists. From 1756 Kirby was tutor in perspective to the Prince of Wales and soon moved to Kew Green. Both men obtained royal offices. Hogarth was appointed Sergeant-Painter to the King in 1757, when John Thornhill resigned through ill health. George III, Kirby's former pupil, appointed Kirby Clerk of Works to Kew Palace in 1759. Hogarth particularly enjoyed this new status and found the numerous contracts it brought very profitable.

Joshua Kirby designed and built St George's Chapel, Brentford, in 1762. His daughter, Sarah, married James Trimmer, who probably supplied the bricks for this project. In adulthood, Sarah remembered meeting Hogarth as a little girl. She pioneered Sunday schools for poor children and wrote children's books. Kirby's Suffolk friend, the artist Thomas Gainsborough, was buried beside him at St Anne's, Kew.

Though Hogarth enjoyed his royal connections, he delighted in the company of people from every walk of life. He and Jane had no children, but welcomed children from the Foundling Hospital to stay in Chiswick, where it is said that they were given mulberry pies.

A tiny curving stair leads to the attic under the roof, where there were two dormitory-style bedrooms. The sloping ceilings were plastered then, but this was not renewed when bomb damage from 1940 was repaired. Both the Hogarths' servants and the visiting children probably slept there. Hogarth's portrait of his servants' heads was painted with great affection. Jane kept it, and it was listed in the sale catalogue of her effects after her death.

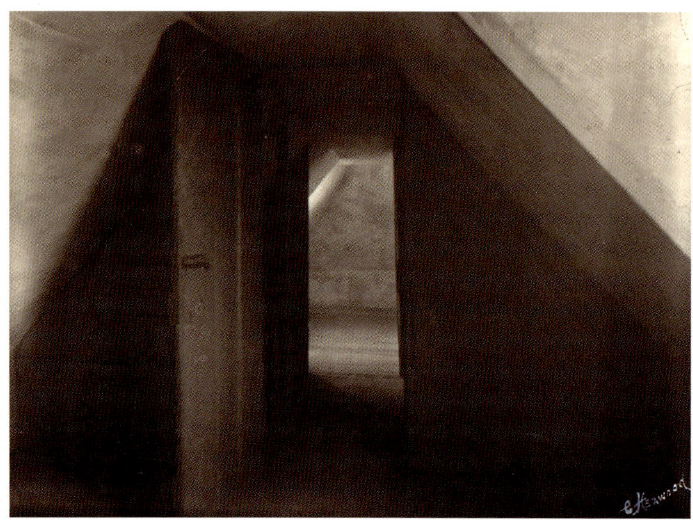

◀ An atmospheric photograph by Charles Henwood showing the empty attics, about 1890.

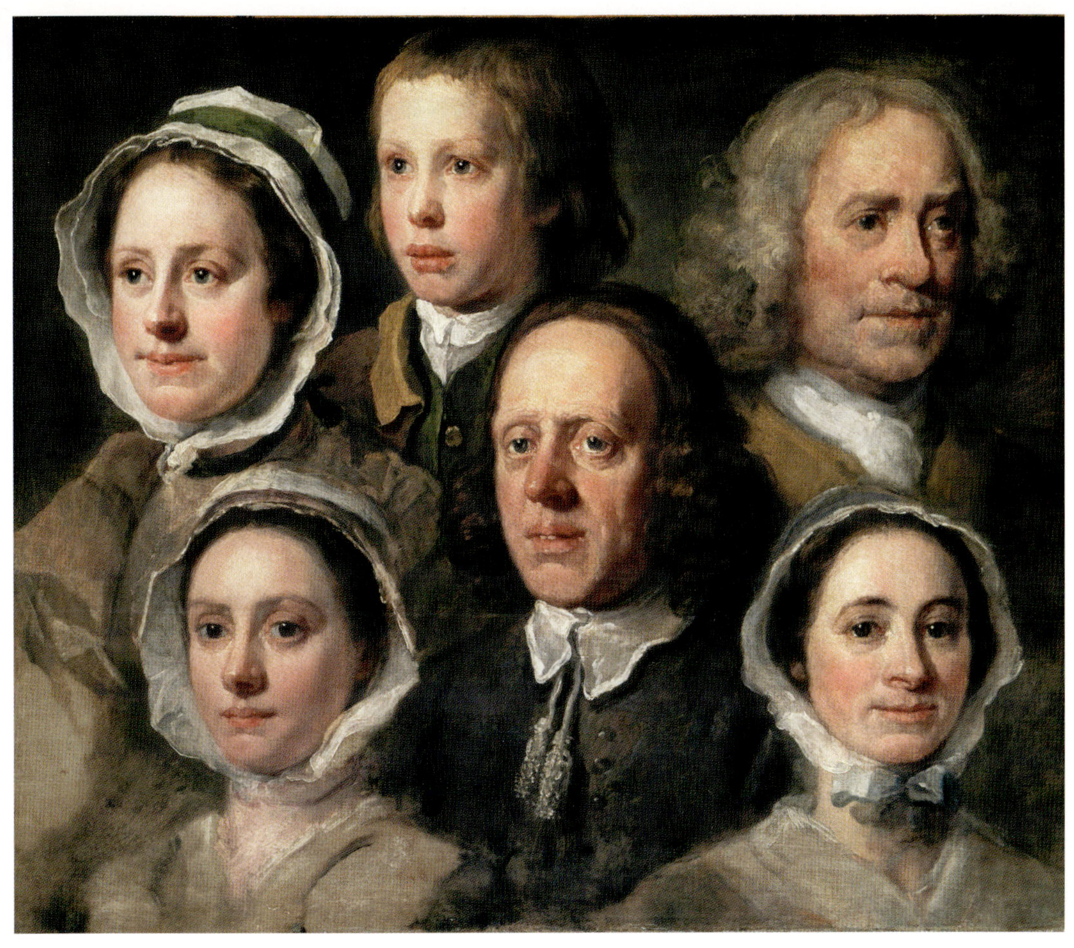

There is no clear record of the servants' names. One could be the George Ellson who shakily signed Hogarth's will in 1764. Jane amended her will in May 1789 to leave Charles Stilewell £20 'if he is still with me at the time of my death'. Some sources name the elderly servants as Ben Ives and Mrs Chappell, while Sir Richard Phillips remembered seeing Jane as an old lady being wheeled to church in Chiswick by her grey-haired servant Samuel, possibly the boy in the picture, grown older.

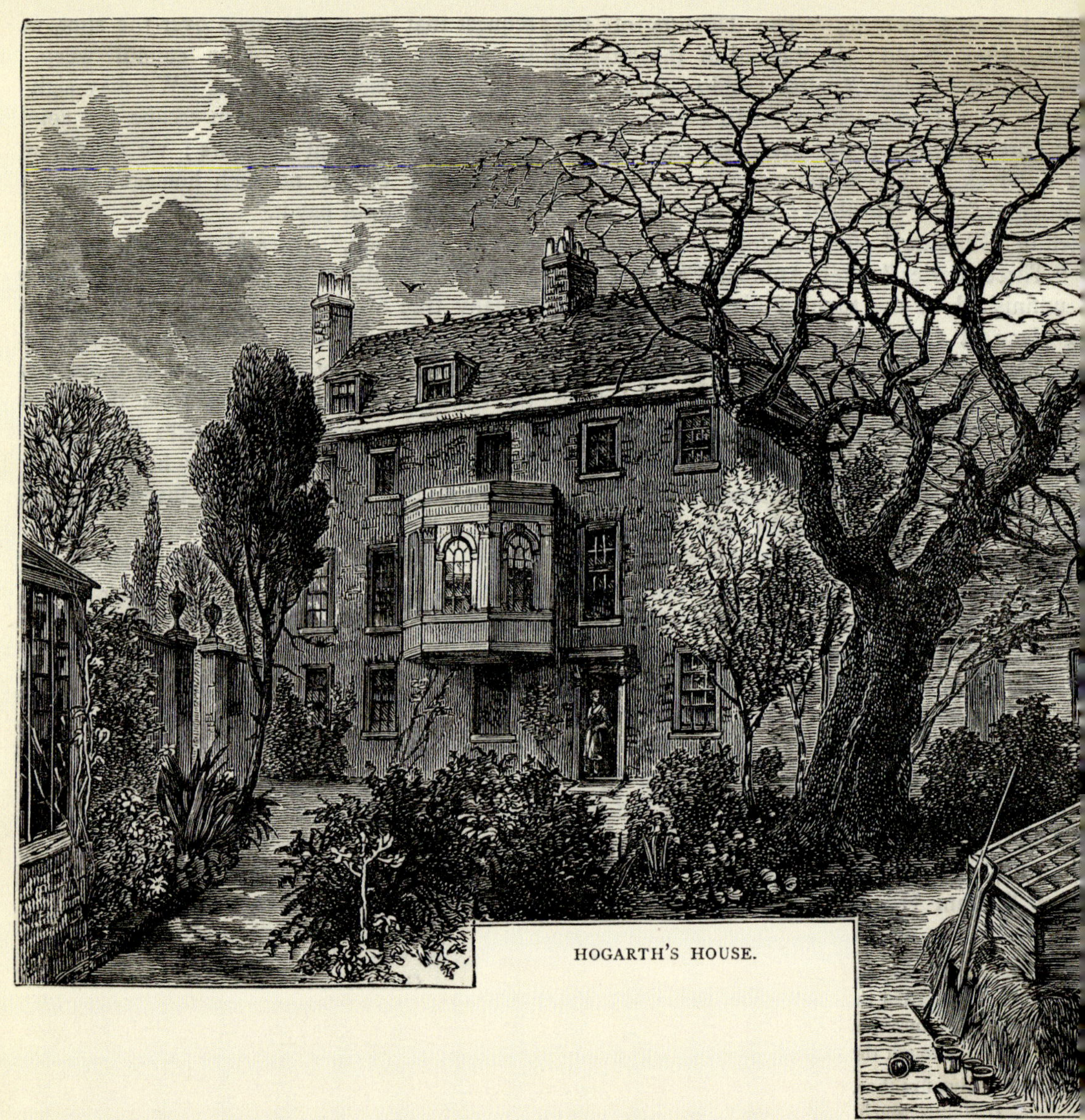

HOGARTH'S HOUSE.

▲ A view from the 1870s, showing
the mulberry tree and the nursery
gardener's small glasshouse,
garden tools and cold frame.

1814–1900

'An excellent garden walled round … in which is also a fine walnut and mulberry tree'

From an advertisement for the sale of the house
in *The Morning Chronicle*, 1814

Loveday's heirs used *The Morning Chronicle* of 29 April 1814 to advertise 'a small but highly respectable House, well known as the Residence of the celebrated Hogarth, pleasantly situated at Chiswick, in an excellent garden walled round, well planted, in which is also a fine walnut and mulberry tree; chaise house and offices'. Henry Francis Cary (1772–1844), the new Curate at St Nicholas' Church, wrote to a friend for advice on rowing on the Thames and moved in with his family that summer.

A memoir compiled by one of his sons provides detailed information about Cary, including letters, poetry and extracts from the diary where he recorded everything he read. The son of a soldier, Cary was born in Gibraltar and hoped to join the army himself. But his grandfather and great-grandfather were both clergymen in Ireland, and he was persuaded to go into the Church. He married Jane Ormsby of Dublin in 1796, and they had five sons and two daughters.

When their six-year-old daughter, Harriet, died of typhus in 1807, Cary had a mental breakdown. In 1817 their daughter Jane, whom Cary had taught French, Italian and Spanish, died from tuberculosis at seventeen, and he wrote a touching sonnet to both lost daughters. Cary had been planning to take Jane to a warmer climate for her health and had resigned from St

Nicholas'. He now obtained the post of Curate at the Savoy Chapel in the Strand, close to the old Lutheran chapel. Another son, born in 1817, raised Cary's spirits; this child was obsessed with London theatre, reciting details of performers and all the shows advertised in the newspapers.

While still at school in 1788, Cary had some poetry published, and he corresponded with Anna Seward, the poet, who encouraged his writing. Besides his duties as a clergyman Cary was carefully translating Dante's works. At first this sold poorly, but while walking with his sons on the beach at Littlehampton and declaiming Homer out loud he met the poet Samuel Taylor Coleridge, in whom he found a champion. Coleridge's praise for Cary's translation, and a favourable review from Italian poet Ugo Foscolo, both in 1818, led to sales of a thousand copies in three months. In the early 1820s Cary was writing articles, mostly for *The London Magazine*, to earn money for his sons' education. Here he became part of a writers' circle that included Charles

▶ A watercolour of about 1825 showing Church Street and St Nicholas' Church, with ferryman in the foreground.

▶▼ A sketch of Henry Francis Cary by his son Francis Henry Cary, published in Judge Henry Cary's memoir of their father.

▼ In the 1830s new streets had appeared north of Hogarth's House, and housing development advanced along the main roads.

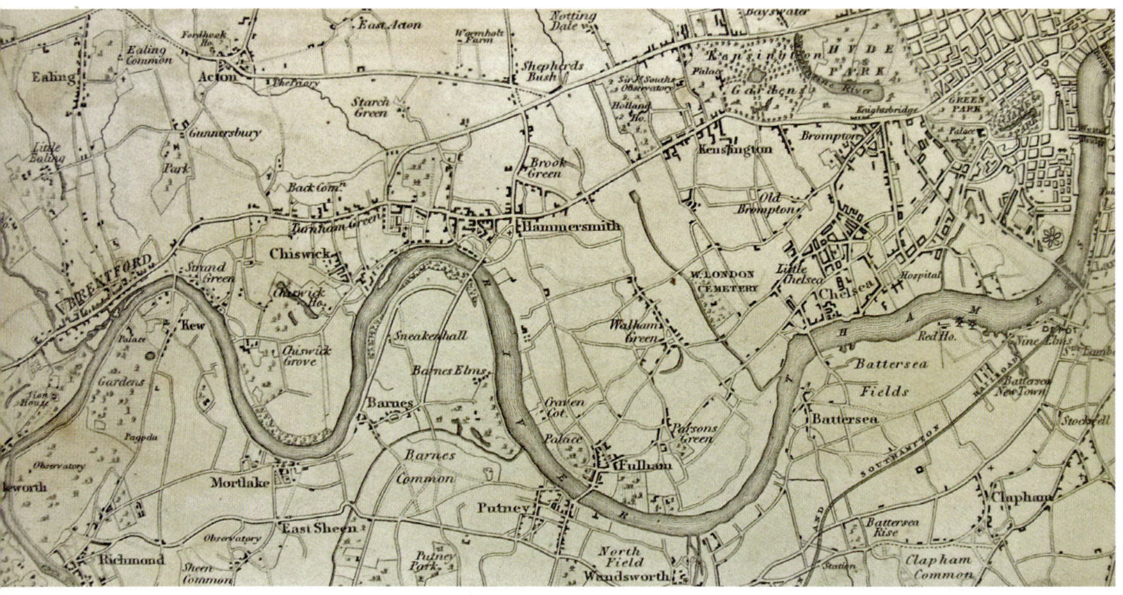

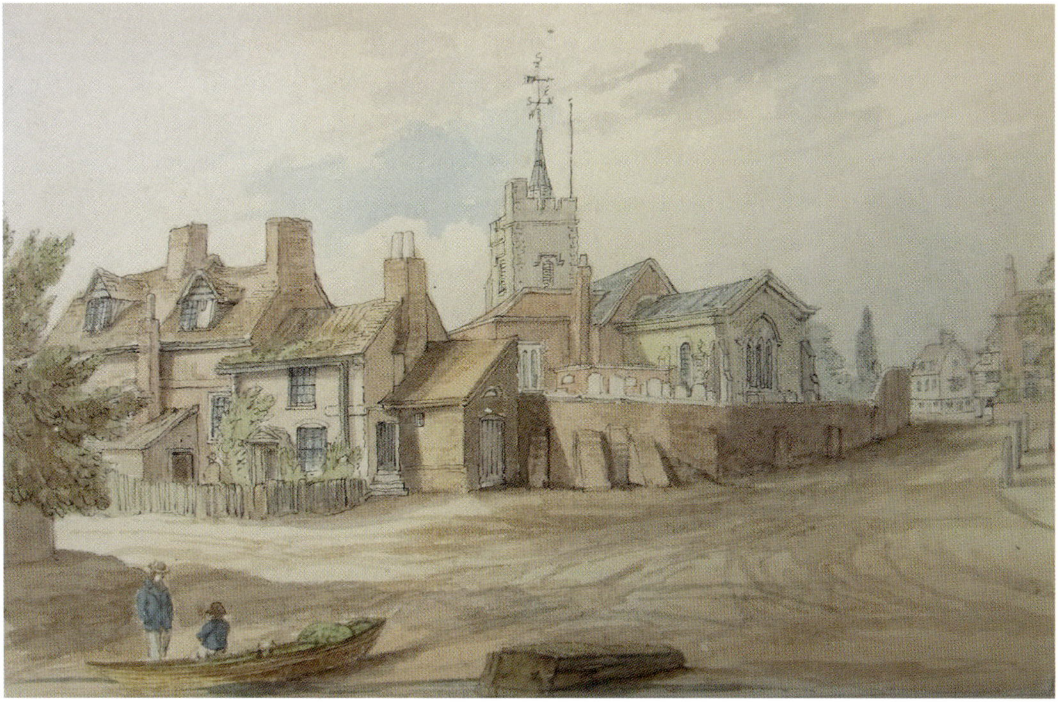

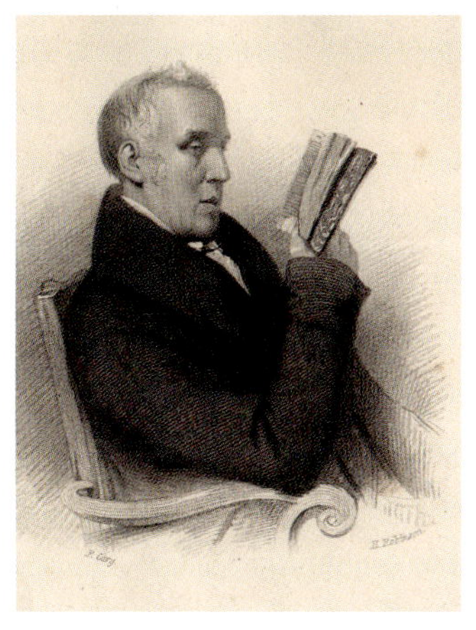

Lamb, William Hazlitt, Thomas de Quincey, John Clare and Thomas Hood. From 1826 Cary was the British Museum's Assistant Keeper of Printed Books, with an apartment there. Hogarth's House became a second home again, until Cary's wife died in 1832. Observing his fragile mental health, the British Museum gave him leave of absence to travel to Italy with one of his sons. The house was sold.

When five years later Cary was passed over for promotion – the Museum thought extra responsibility would put too much pressure upon him – he abruptly resigned, writing a furious letter to the press. He spent his last years revising his translations, living near his son's Bloomsbury art school, where John Everett Millais and Dante Gabriele Rossetti (son of his father's friend Gabriele) were trained. He was buried in Westminster Abbey in 1844.

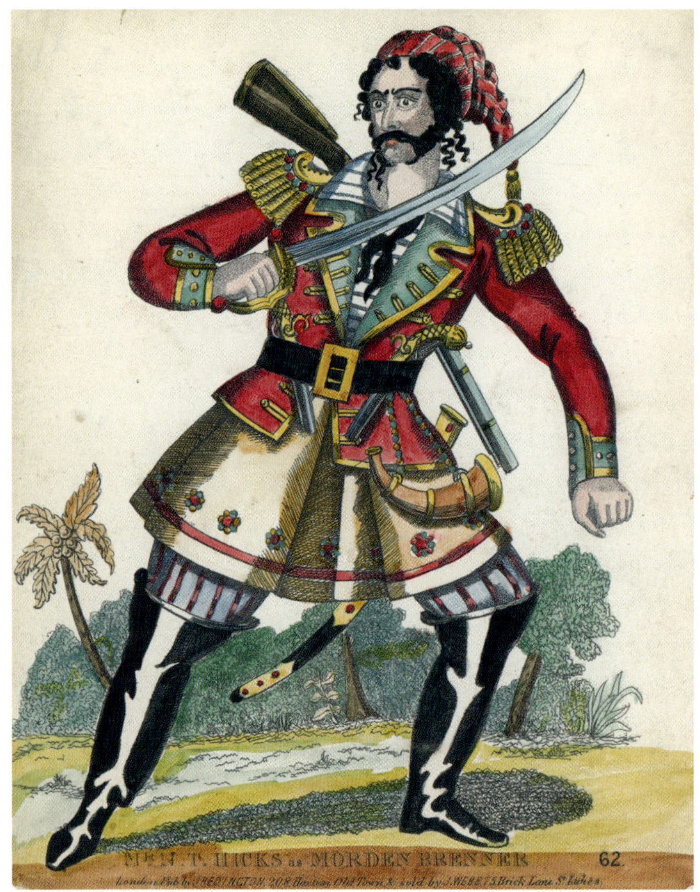

The Wickstead family bought the house. The area around it was changing, with new streets of working-class housing to the north and industry to the east. John Wickstead migrated to Australia in 1840, where he ran the Union Hotel and general store in Fremantle. He left the house in Samuel Thoady's care, but he too left for Australia in 1850. The house remained in the Wicksteads' ownership until 1890, let to a succession of tenants. The melodramatic actor, Newton Treen 'Brayvo' Hicks, lived there with his second wife from about 1865 until he died in 1873.

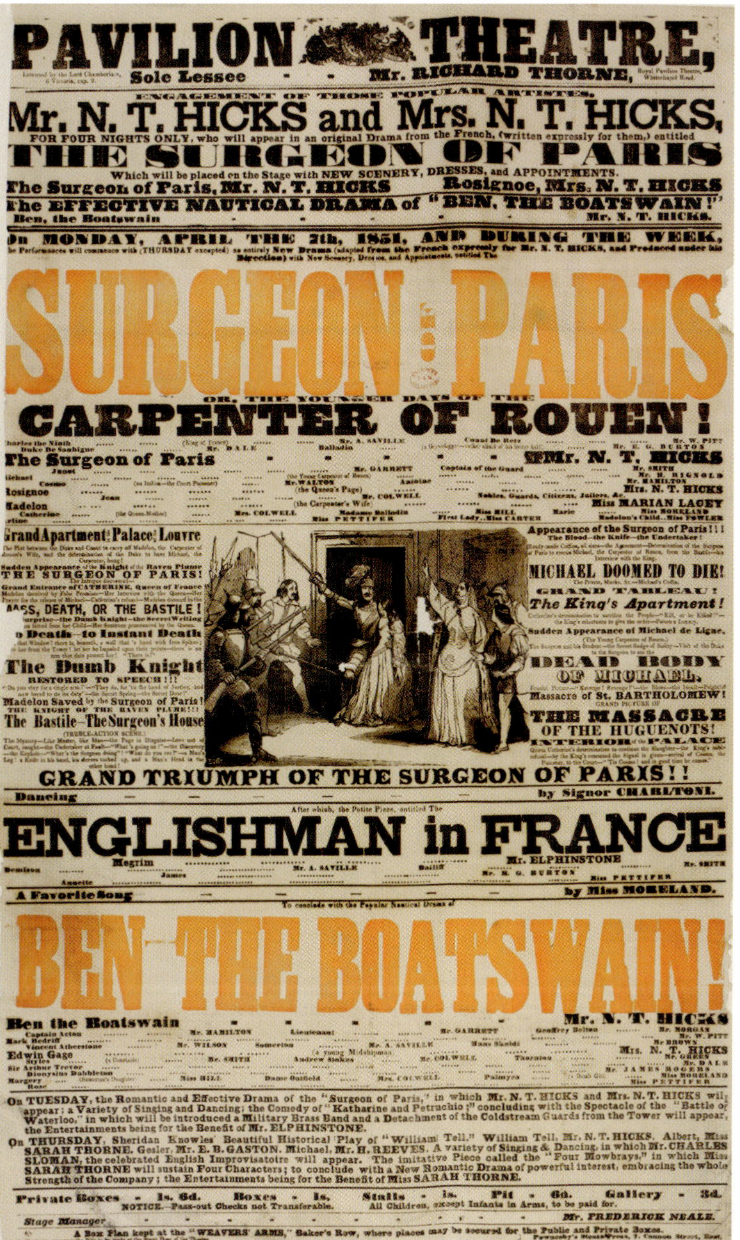

A playbill for the Pavilion Theatre, Whitechapel Road, advertising performances by 'those popular artistes' Mr & Mrs N. T. Hicks, 1851.

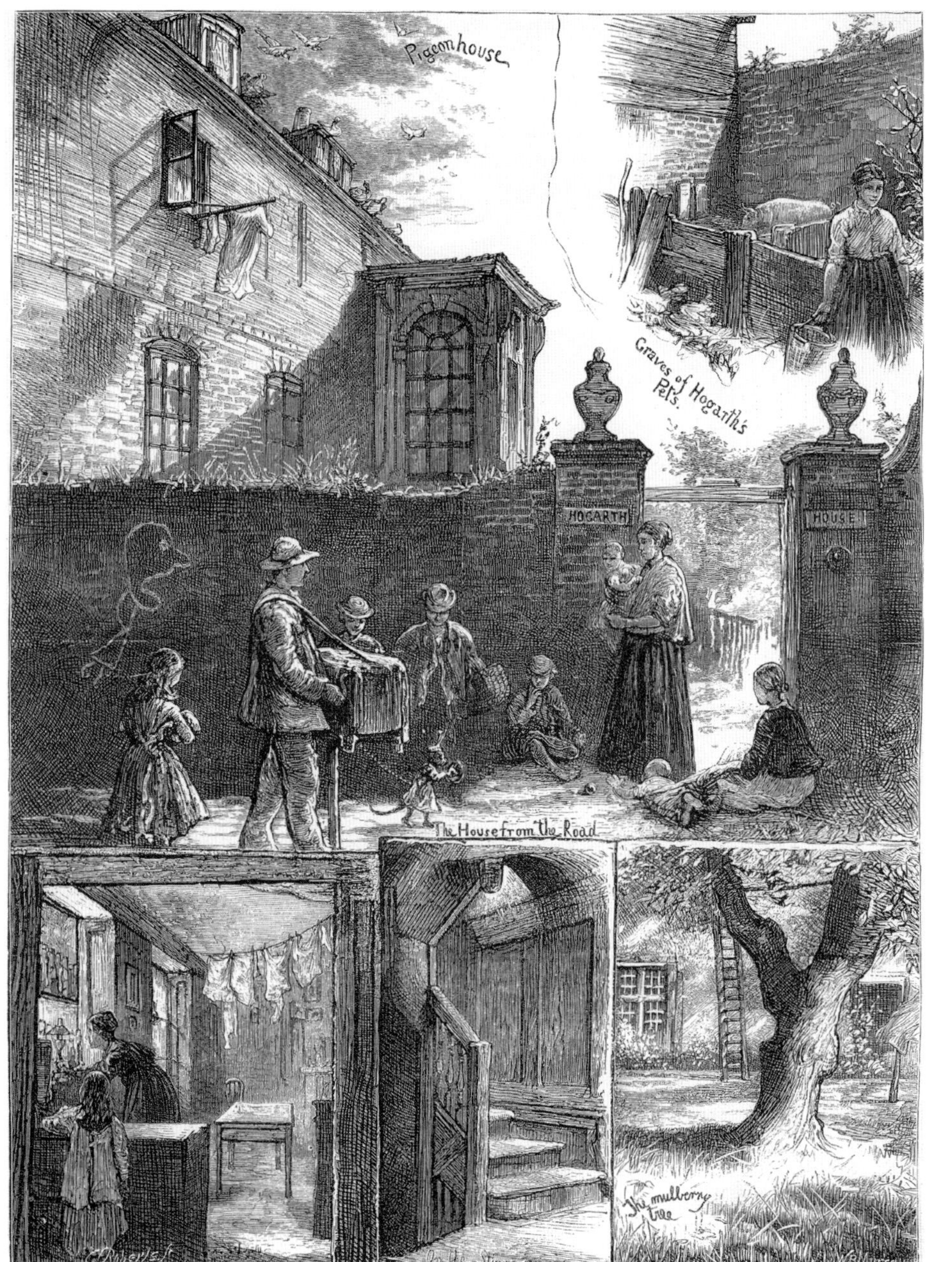

Pigeonhouse
Graves of Hogarth's Pets.
HOGARTH
HOUSE
The House from the Road
The mulberry tree

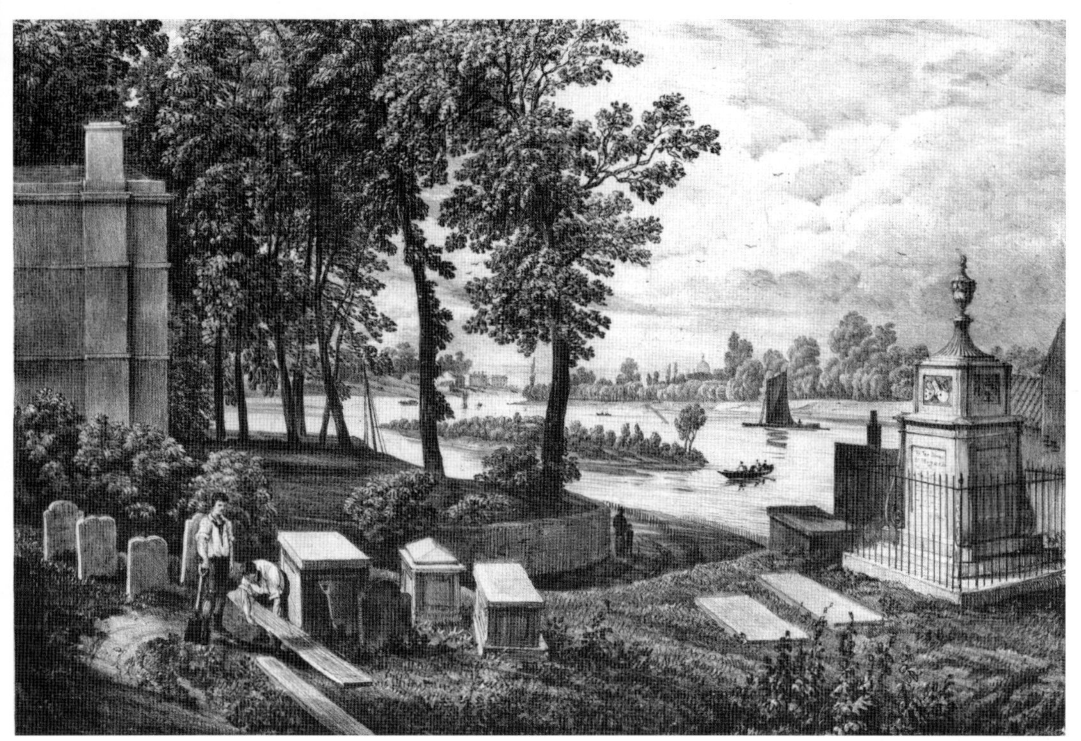

▲ Hogarth's celebrity continued after his death. This lithograph of 1823 provides a memento of a visit to the family monument.

◄ The house, the mulberry tree, Mrs Clack with her pigs and also in the shop with her daughter – an illustration from *The Daily Graphic*, 1874.

A painting chair said to have been Hogarth's was sold in the 1860s, and soon after Hicks' death the painting room was pulled down, or fell down. Two families – the Clacks and the Coles – moved into the house. An 1874 newspaper report bemoaning the neglect of the home of a famous man prompted a letter in response stating that Mr Clack looked after it well and showed visitors round. By 1881 Mrs Clack was widowed, living with her mother and small daughter; she kept pigs and ran a shop from the dining room. George Coles, his wife and small children shared the house. He worked the garden as a nurseryman.

In the 1870s the painter Charles J. Staniland (1838–1916) lived at Hogarth Cottage, next door. He sketched the house with Hogarth in the garden for *The Illustrated London News*. The art critic, F. G. Stephens, who had recently written *Artists at Home*, tried unsuccessfully to persuade the Royal Academy to buy the house in 1886.

The area became increasingly industrial, with shipbuilding works, two breweries and the Chiswick Polish Company's factory nearby. At The Cedars in Burlington Lane lived Henry Dawson, landscape painter, with his sons, Alfred and Charles. Accomplished painters and engravers who exhibited at the Royal Academy, they ran their Typographic Etching Company from the Hogarth Works in Short Road. It specialised in plates for high-quality reproductions of works of art. Emery Walker was their apprentice and eventually their manager. His house on Hammersmith Terrace is also open to visitors; in the garden is a vine said to be from a cutting of one at Hogarth's House.

At the end of 1890 Alfred bought Hogarth's House from John Wickstead's granddaughter. He later wrote: 'The great aim has been a real restoration to its original condition, not removing or destroying an atom that could be kept in position. There were serious uncouth additions made by subtenants during the last 40 years … these were removed.' John Allgrove rented the house along with part of the garden of The Cedars and ran the Hogarth

▼ The Cedars from the garden, engraved by Alfred Dawson for his memoir of his father, Henry Dawson.

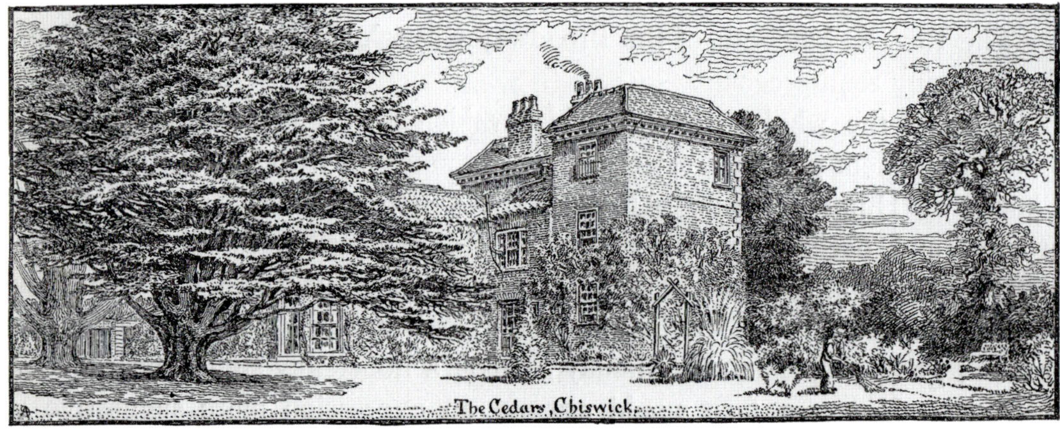

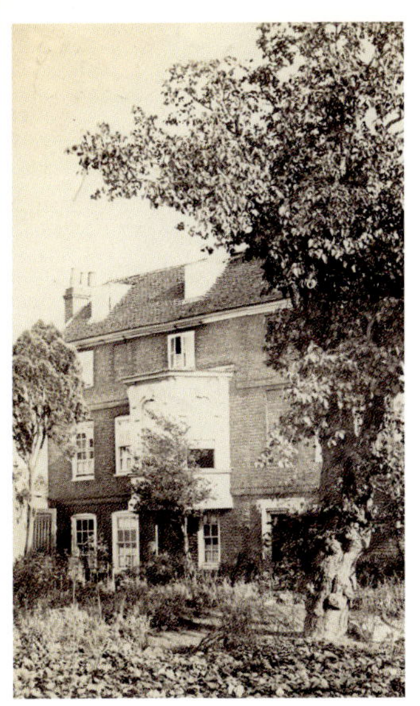

▲ Probably the oldest surviving photograph of the house and mulberry tree, with Mr Clack's name painted on the gate, 1870s.

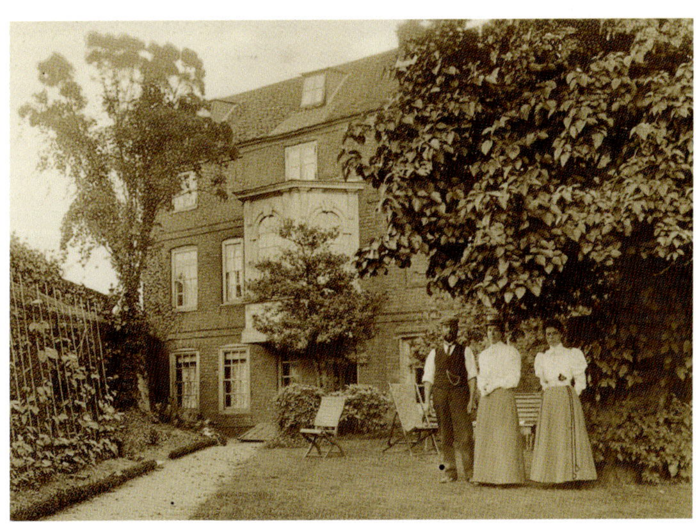

▶ John Allgrove, nursery gardener, and his wife, Elizabeth, with a visitor in the garden, 1890s.

House Nursery there during the 1890s. In 1900 Dawson sold Hogarth's House to T. H. Currie, an auctioneer and estate agent. In March 1901 *The Daily Telegraph* carried the news that the house and garden were likely to make way for 'the construction of villa residences'.

Though the idea of preserving artists' houses as museums was a new one, numerous letters appeared in the national and local press, anxious that the house should be saved. That summer large numbers of visitors appeared, expecting to visit the house.

The Hogarth's House Preservation Committee was launched that May, chaired by designer George Haité; most of the members were literary and artistic men, several of whom lived in Bedford Park, the artistic suburb nearby.

Each member subscribed one guinea to cover campaign expenses such as printing and sending out 5,000 circulars. They approached men of wealth and wrote to numerous newspapers but they raised only £472. Most of this came from their friends and contacts, and only £12 had come from Chiswick people. Demolition seemed inevitable.

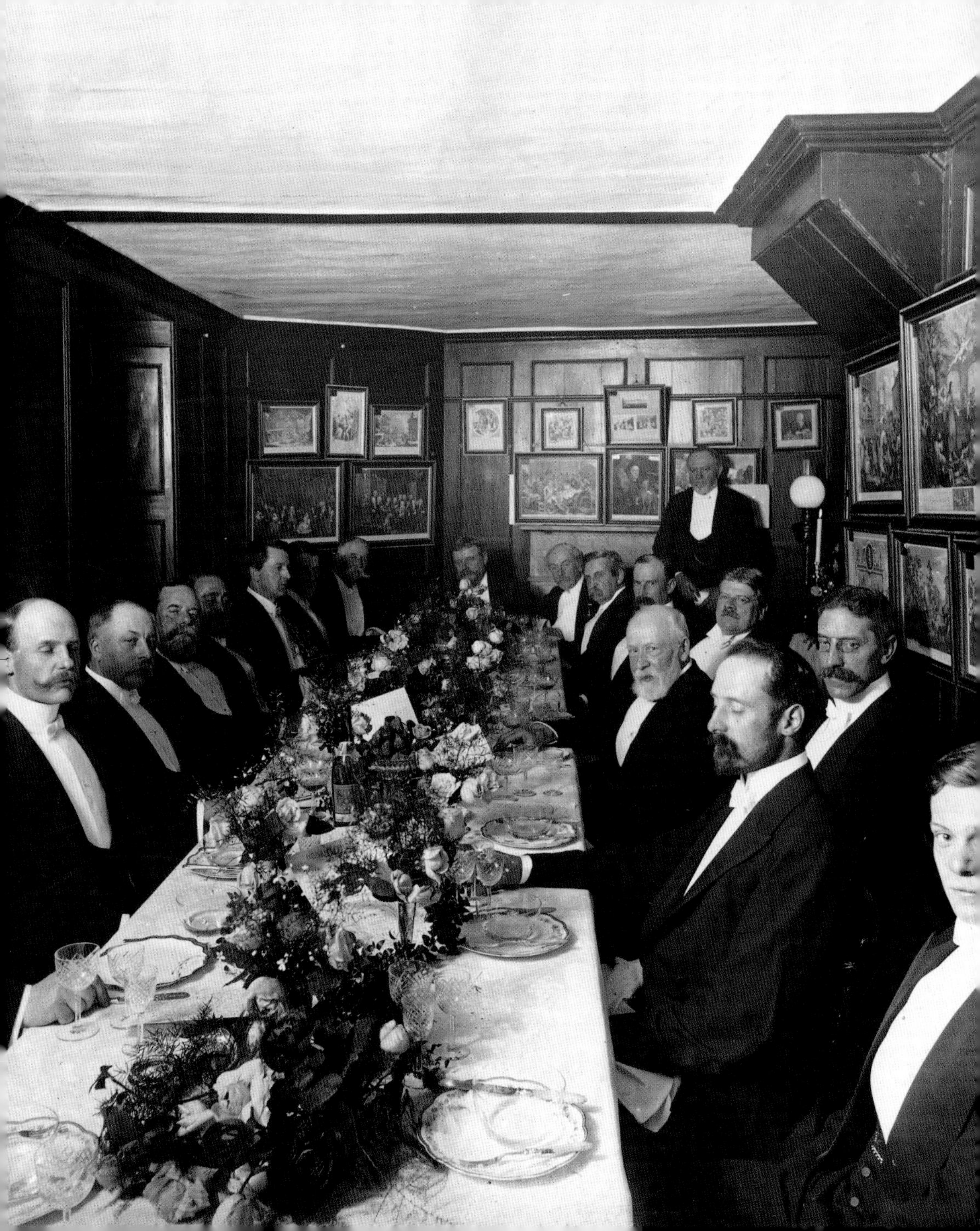

Since 1900

'Historical & Interesting Premises … occupied by the great Satirist Artist, Wm. Hogarth'

From the sales particulars for Hogarth's House, 1901

Shortly before the auction in November 1901, *The Chiswick Times* appealed for 'some public-spirited philanthropic resident of the district to step into the breach'. Lieutenant Colonel William Shipway of Grove House, Chiswick, did so, much to the surprise of the local newspaper, and bought Hogarth's House for £1,500. A wealthy man, he left £93,000 at his death in 1928. Shortly before Shipway opened the house to visitors, he held a dinner there for artists, politicians and museum directors, where he paid tribute to his wife, Helen, for insisting that he should buy it.

Shipway engaged architect Frederick S. Peel to restore the structure, used the Chiswick Art-Workers' Guild to make replica furniture from Hogarth's works, assembled a collection of prints and took the photos for the first guidebook. In 1902 he took a Mr Percy to court for undermining the south-east corner of the house by extracting gravel from the site. The distorted panelling in the first floor room furthest from the road still shows the subsidence. Shipway opened the house to visitors in 1904.

Shipway may have bought the house to re-establish his social standing, having been defrauded by a bogus genealogist who forged historical evidence for his family tree in 1896. The subsequent court case, widely covered in the national newspapers, was humiliating – and it was W. P. W. Phillimore, a historian and

◀ Helen Shipway's photograph of the dinner. Sir Lawrence Alma-Tadema heads the table, and Shipway, with handlebar moustache, is beside him.

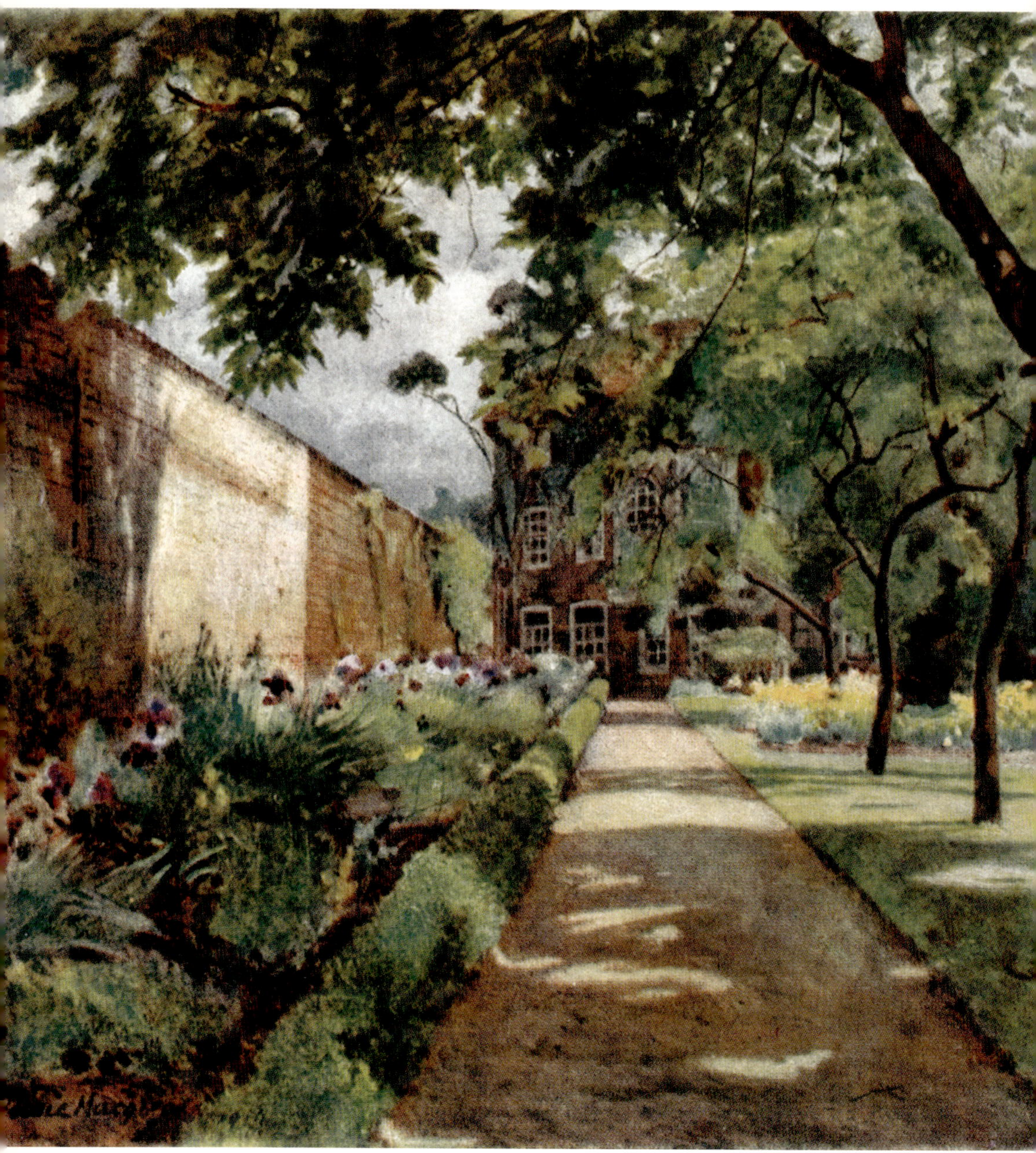

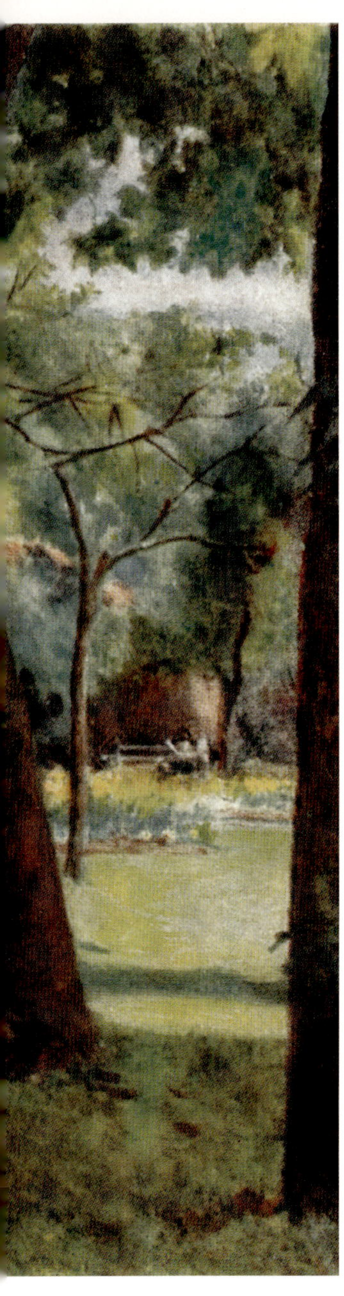

Chiswick member of the Preservation Committee, who called in the police. Shipway had succeeded in saving the house where Phillimore and his friends could not.

The publicity about saving the house led John Leighton (1822–1912) to promise his copy of Hogarth's self-portrait should the campaign succeed. A co-founder of *The Graphic* and a prolific designer of bookbindings, he seems to have fulfilled his promise – the collection includes a Victorian copy of the painting. Admirers of Hogarth have since given items to the house, including books, prints, furniture and Hogarth's printing plates for the *Hudibras* series (see page 48).

Shipway made a charitable gift of the house and contents to Middlesex County Council in 1909. Custodians lived in the house rent-free in return for showing visitors around and caring for house and garden. Shipway had daffodils planted beneath the mulberry and purple irises behind a low box hedge along the old path; this planting echoed the Arts and Crafts style of the 1904 furnishings and the first guidebook.

Kelly's Directories list John Thomas Airey as the first custodian in 1904, followed by Frank J. Bateman in 1905. No further names are listed until 1933, when Albert Stafford Diddams moved in. A nurse specialising in the care of the mentally ill, he worked at the Tuke family's private asylum at Chiswick House, where he met his wife. She opened the house to visitors and cared for their two daughters and a son.

When the house was about to close for refurbishment in late 2008, two of the Diddams children visited . Though very young when they moved away, they remembered playing in the garden where their father, who was a great enthusiast for tulips, also grew vegetables. Their mother cooked mulberries and plums from the old orchard trees.

◄ A watercolour of the garden in spring
by Jessie Macgregor for her book *Gardens of Celebrities and Celebrated Gardens*, 1913.

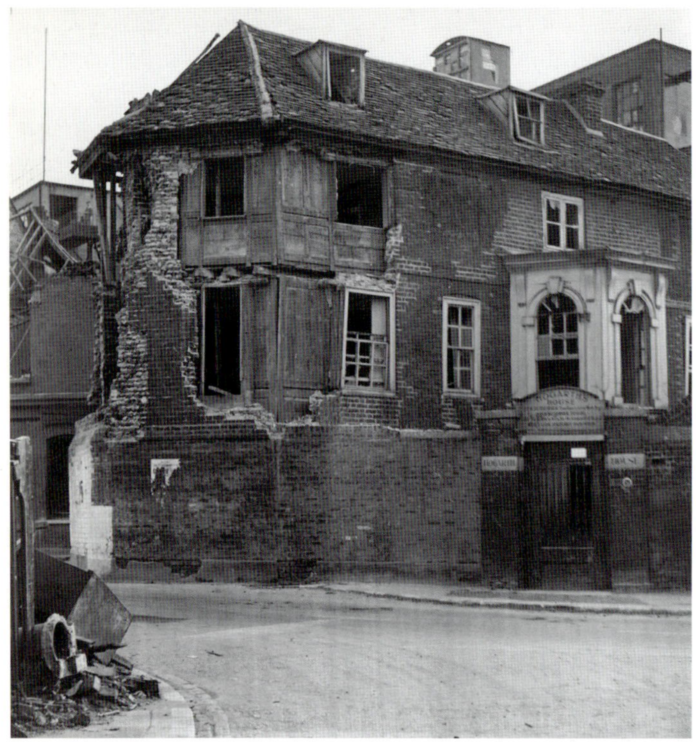

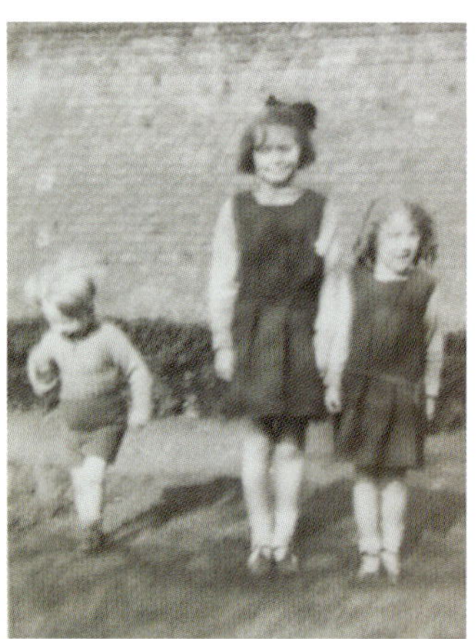

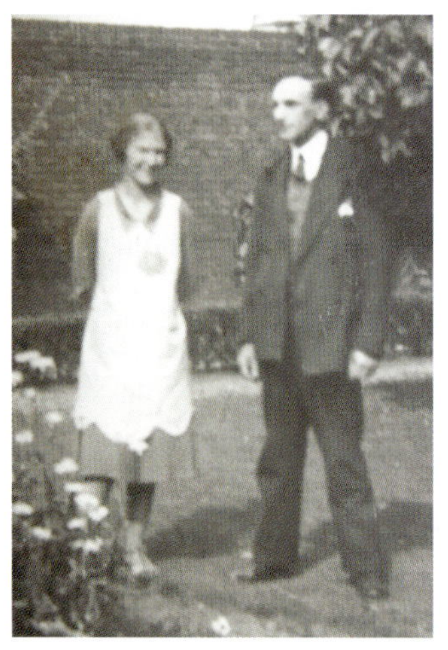

The Diddams family were sheltering in the cellar with neighbours when a nearby landmine blasted the house in 1940. Water from the row of fire buckets in the hall cascaded on them through gaps in the floorboards. They were taken to the robust concrete Hogarth Laundry next door for the rest of the night. The house was uninhabitable – the north wall and the kitchen wing were shattered and the old mulberry tree badly damaged.

The County Council boarded up the damaged house and took the museum contents to Chiswick Library, but some of the Diddams' possessions, including their gas fires, had already been stolen. The council's engineers recommended demolishing the northern end for safety reasons; instead steel ropes were inserted to strengthen the interior.

The Chiswick Polish works expanded across the site of The Cedars right up to Hogarth's House. Betty Severn worked there in the early 1940s and visited Hogarth's House soon after it re-opened in 2011. She told a remarkable story. Chiswick Polish intended to buy the bomb-damaged house for further expansion. Betty was lodging at Red Lion House on Chiswick Mall where her landlord happened to be John McGregor, an architect involved with the Society for the Protection of Ancient Buildings. She told him of the threat to Hogarth's House and he swung into action.

McGregor advised on temporary repairs in 1943, but five years later the county architect reported that the walls were beginning to lean. In 1951 funds were found for full repairs, creating a second floor custodian's flat and rebuilding the kitchen wing as an exhibition gallery. It reopened in September 1951, when *The Brentford Times* reported McGregor as being 'well pleased as he had thought that the building was too far gone'.

Already surrounded by industrial buildings on three sides, the house survived the transformation of Hogarth Lane into the A4

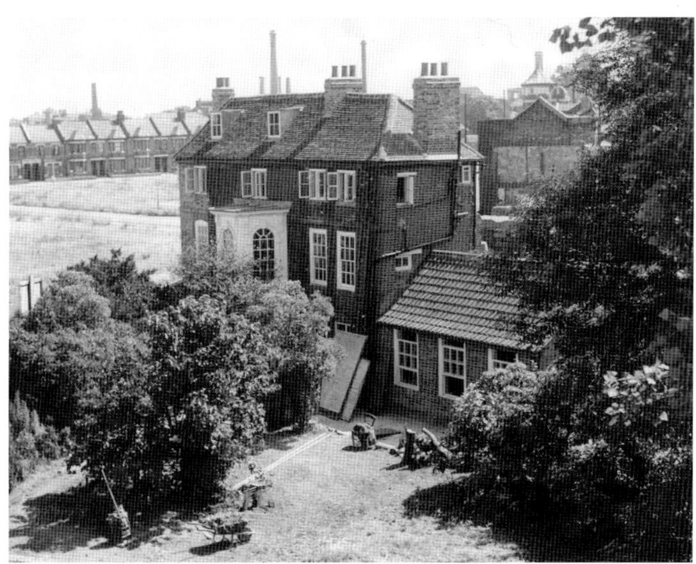

► Repairs in progress, 1951. Beyond the wall bombed housing has been cleared for the construction of the new road.

trunk road in the 1950s and its later expansion into a six-lane dual carriageway. Designation as a Grade I listed building came too late to prevent the construction of the substantial Hogarth Laundry to the west in the 1930s, and seems not to have influenced the design of the Hogarth Business Park in the 1980s, whose only benefit was the allocation of parking spaces there for Hogarth's House visitors.

When the Greater London Council was created in 1965, Middlesex County Council's interest in the house was transferred to the London Borough of Hounslow, which managed it as part of the Library Service without any curatorial expertise. During a cost-saving exercise in 1984 the then Borough Librarian proposed selling off the house, as he thought it had too few visitors to justify opening it.

James Wisdom, Chairman of the Brentford & Chiswick Local History Society, ran a vigorous campaign in its defence and gained considerable public support. He assembled the key Hogarth experts to advise on re-display, found a museum designer to estimate the costs and persuaded Reckitt and Colman to allocate £30,000 towards the works. The house was not sold, but the Borough Librarian refused the offer of expertise and funding.

For the 300th anniversary of Hogarth's birth in 1997, the interior was refurbished. With grants from the Heritage Lottery Fund, the Pilgrim Trust and the Esmée Fairbairn Foundation, many of the prints were conserved, the panelling was patched, the interior was repainted and large information panels were installed. Visitors were enthusiastic, and their numbers rose.

In 1999, to mark the Millennium, the Chiswick Traders' Association commissioned a statue of Hogarth from Jim Matthieson. They raised £82,000, with many personal donations from enthusiastic supporters and two events at Chiswick Town Hall. Four generous gifts came from the Hogarth Health Club, the developers of the new Chiswick Park offices,

▶ The dining room of about 1770, restored after the fire in 2009, painted pale grey, with a maquette for the Hogarth statue, 2011.

▶ Hogarth's bedroom, painted mid-grey, with 1904 replica furniture, clothes from his 1757 self-portrait in the closet and prints, 2011.

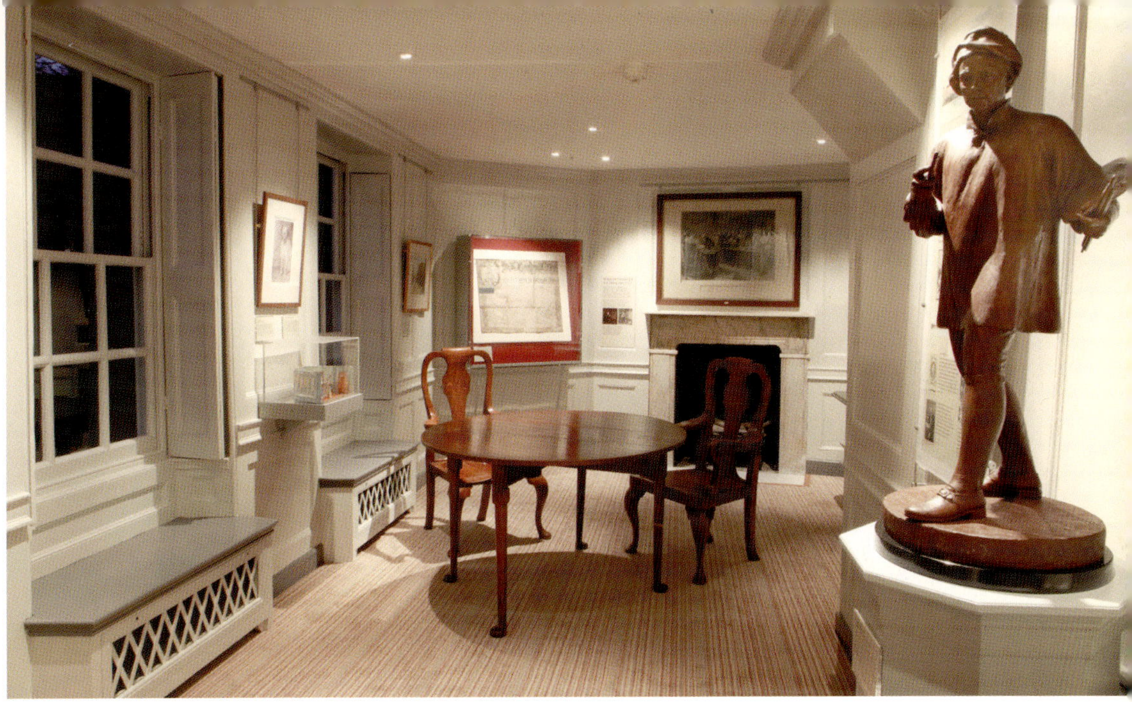

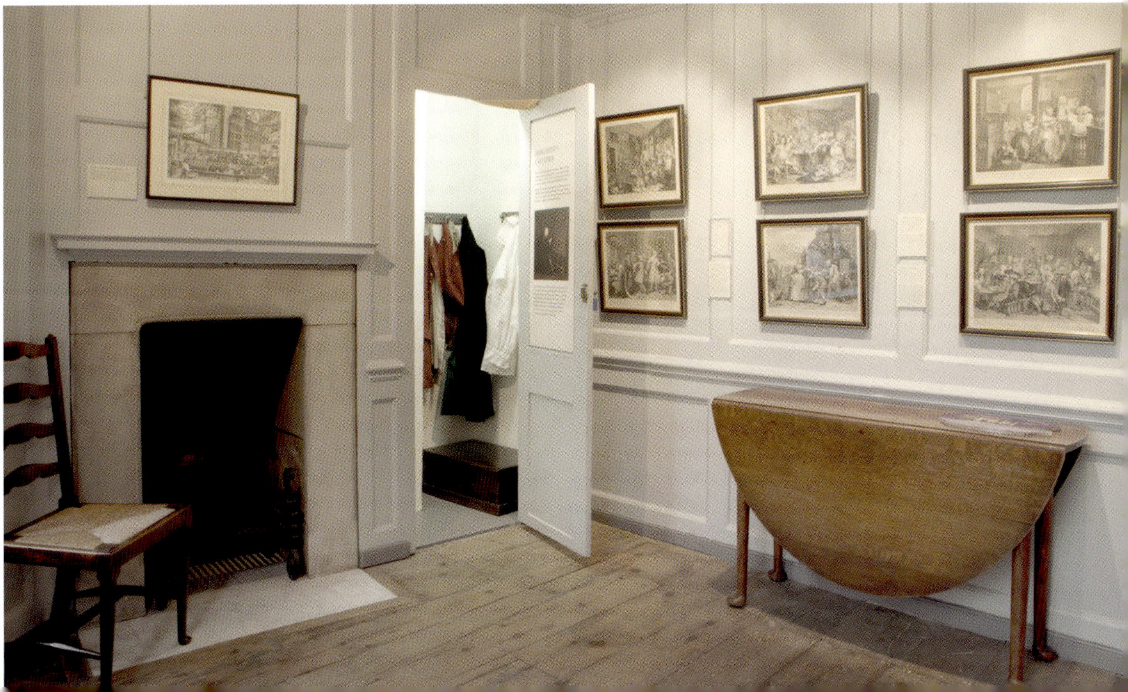

Sainsbury's supermarkets and David Hockney, patron of the appeal. The statue was unveiled in 2001 by Ian Hislop, with David Hockney's help, and the pug at his heels was unveiled by Leaha James, a pupil at William Hogarth School.

In 2002 the fund-raising committee became a registered charity, the William Hogarth Trust, with the objective of raising awareness and understanding of the life, work and interests of William Hogarth. It has raised funds to purchase items for the Hogarth's House collection. Working with Hounslow officers, including the long-standing custodian, Les Channer, and members of the Local History Society, it also put on exhibitions and a programme of events to mark the centenary of the museum in 2004. The new visitors these attracted wanted to understand how the house worked as a home, and who else had lived there beside the Hogarths.

To support further improvements, the Trust drafted for Hounslow Council a grant application to the Heritage Lottery Fund, to refurbish the entire structure for the first time since 1951 and to re-present the house to reach a wider audience. With funds from HLF, the John & Ruth Howard Charitable Trust, the Old Chiswick Protection Society and the William Hogarth Trust, the work has been completed. The house closed in September 2008, and building conservation work began early in 2009. Two weeks after the contractors left, an electrical fire caused serious damage to the dining room and staircase; fortunately, local firemen saved the house from destruction.

Work resumed early in 2011 and this time was completed successfully. With new displays and a study room and office in the former custodian's flat on the second floor, Hogarth's House was reopened in November 2011 by Dara Ò Briain, a modern satirist living in Chiswick.

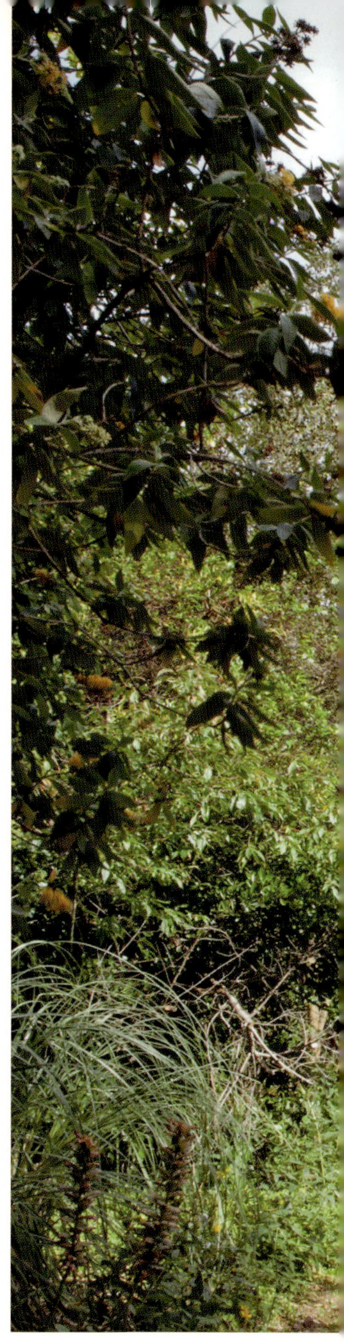

▶ The newly refurbished House in 2011, with new mortar revealing the junction between the 1750 extension and the original.

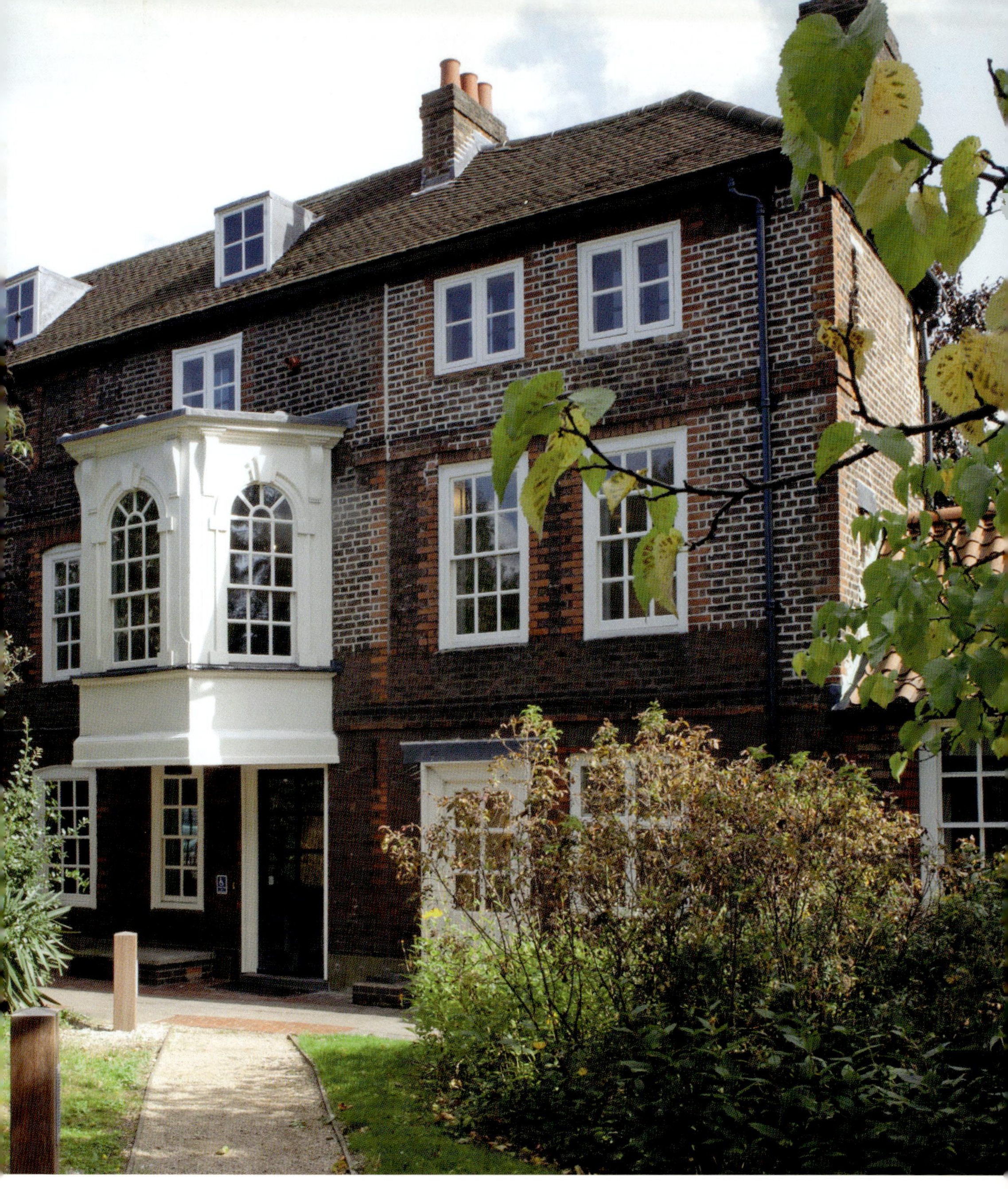

We are grateful to the following for permission
to use images from their collections.

Aberdeen Art Gallery and Museums Collections:
    pages 19 (bottom), 20 (bottom), 21 (right)
BBC News website / Paul Kerley: page 48
Brentford & Chiswick Local History Society: page 14
Bridgeman Art Library / Cincinatti Art Museum:
    pages 12–13
Diddams family: page 42 (top right, bottom)
Hounslow Council: pages 4, 5, 6, 8, 9, 18, 19 (top),
    20 (top), 23, 26, 28, 30, 31, 34, 35, 36, 37, 38, 40–41,
    42 (top left), 43
Katri Salonen: pages 45, 46–47
Look and Learn: page 32
National Portrait Gallery: back cover, page 1
St Mary's Lutheran Church, Bloomsbury / Photoview:
    page 16
Tate Britain: page 27
Trustees of the British Museum: inside front cover,
    pages 2, 5 (top right), 7, 11, 17, 22, 24
V&A Theatre & Performance: page 33
William Hogarth Trust: page 25
Yale Center for British Art: pages 10, 21 (left)

Front cover: *Hogarth's House*, watercolour
by Thomas Matthew Rooke, 1897.

Rear cover: Hogarth's self-portrait of 1757.

Front cover flap: Detail from an engraving of
The Painter and his Pug, Hogarth's self-portrait
of 1745.

Rear cover flap: Detail from an illustration in
Old & New London, 1878 (see page 28).

Inside front cover: Etching of 1782 from a
sketch by Hogarth, *c.*1750, showing his house
behind a high wall.

Inside rear cover: Detail from an engraving of
Chiswick from Harrison's *History of London*, 1775
(see page 18).

▶ Detail of one of Hogarth's printing plates
for *Hudibras*.

© Scala Publishers Ltd, 2012
Text © Val Bott, 2012

First published in 2012 by
Scala Publishers Ltd
Northburgh House
10 Northburgh St
London EC1V 0AT
Telephone: +44 (0) 20 7490 9900
www.scalapublishers.com

ISBN: 978-1-85759-754-7

Editor: Esme West
Designer: Yvonne Dedman
Printed and bound in China

10 9 8 7 6 5 4 3 2 1

British Library Cataloguing in Publication Data

A catalogue record for this book is available
from the British Library.

*Hogarth's House and its collection are owned by the
London Borough of Hounslow and managed on its behalf by
Hounslow Community Services for the benefit and pleasure
of its residents and visitors.*

Hogarth's House
Hogarth Lane
Great West Road
London W4 2QN
www.hounslow.info/arts/hogarthshouse

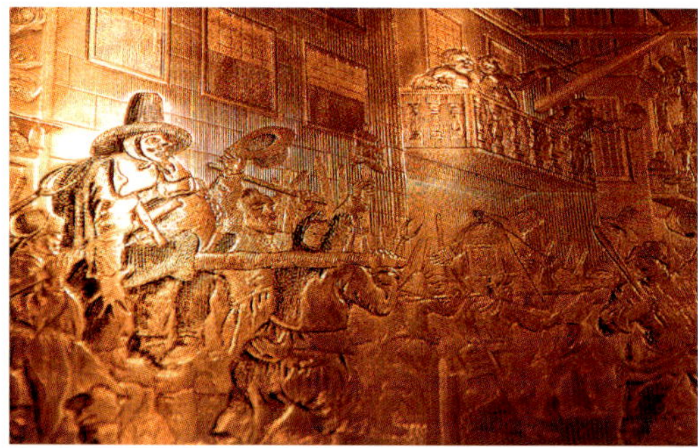